GOTHIC FOR
THE STEAM AGE

GOTHIC FOR THE STEAM AGE

AN ILLUSTRATED BIOGRAPHY OF GEORGE GILBERT SCOTT

GAVIN STAMP

Aurum
Press

First published in Great Britain
2015 by Aurum Press Ltd
74—77 White Lion Street
Islington
London N1 9PF
www.aurumpress.co.uk

ISBN 978 1 78131 124 0

10 9 8 7 6 5 4 3 2 1
2019 2018 2017 2016 2015

Designed by Ashley Western
Printed in China

ENDPAPERS: Detail of the south elevation of Scott's competition-winning design for the Midland Hotel, St Pancras Station, 1865.

FRONTISPIECE: St Giles' Church, Camberwell, London, seen from the west in 2014.

OVERLEAF: George Gilbert Scott in his prime: *carte-de-visite* photograph of the 1860s by J & C Watkins.

ILLUSTRATIONS CREDITS

Aardvark/Alamy page 167.
Jon Arnold/Corbis 179 (left).
Berlin Technischen Universität 86.
Geoff Brandwood 103, 104 (top), 106 (top), 120 (both), 121 (right), 122 (both), 123 (both), 161 (middle & bottom).
Brighton College 160 (top).
British Architectural Library Endpapers, 23 (left), 26 (left), 34-5, 40, 61, 63 (top), 64, 65 (top & bottom), 66, 77, 112 (left), 137 (top left), 176 (bottom).
British Museum 28.
Royal Pavilion & Museum, Brighton & Hove 179 (right).
Church Care Library (Cathedrals and Church Buildings Division), Church House 31, 50 (right), 112 (right), 128, 129, 135 (top), *ditto.*, photos by Gordon Barnes (©English Heritage) 106 (bottom), 111 (right, top & bottom), 114 (all three), 124 (top), 126.
Canadian Centre for Architecture 108 (top).
Country Life 180.
Photopolis (Dundee City Council) 156 (middle).
Fox Photos/Getty Images 141 (top)
Historic England Archive (National Monuments Record) 18, 44, 82 (bottom), 98 (both), 100 (both), 115, 134 (bottom), 137, right top & bottom), 145, 152 (bottom), 153 (bottom right), 176 (top), 177, 178 (bottom), 189, 193 (top), 199.
All SS Church Hillesden 26 (right).
Peter Howell 187.
Lambeth Palace Library (ICBS Archive) 110 (bottom right).
Lancashire County Library & Information Services 155 (right).
Leeds Library & Information Service 48.
Leeds Art Gallery 175.
Toby Melville/Press Association Images 21.
National Archives 178 (top)
National Portrait Gallery 6, 90.
Royal Academy of Arts 68-9.
Royal Collection Trust 146 (bottom) .
Royal Commission on the Ancient & Historical Monuments of Scotland 23 (right).
Royal Commission on the Ancient & Historical Monuments of Wales 188.
Richard Gilbert Scott 84 (all three).
Society of Antiquaries 50 (left).
Dean & Chapter of Westminster 10, 195.
Peter Wheeler/Alamy 190
Andrew Dixon White Architectural Photograph Collection, Division of Rare and Manuscript Collections, Cornell University Library 139, 141 (bottom), 147, 158, 164 (top), 165 (top), 168 (bottom), 194 (bottom), 196 (top), 197.
Adam Woolfitt 151, 153 (top right & bottom left).

All other historical images are from the author's own collection; all other modern photographs were taken by the author.

CONTENTS

Preface

George Gilbert Scott, who became Sir Gilbert Scott, was the most famous and prolific of all Victorian architects. He was responsible for the Albert Memorial in Kensington, a cathedral in Edinburgh, the Universities of Glasgow and Bombay, several college chapels, libraries, hospitals, schools and a jail as well as parish churches and parsonage houses all over Britain. Yet there is, at present, no general study available of Scott's extraordinary career, nor any single publication which illustrates the range of his achievement: hence this book. Scott's was the largest architectural office of its time, producing designs for some eight hundred buildings, monuments and restoration schemes (estimates vary), and only a selection can be included here. All of his major secular works are illustrated – by a combination of old and new photographs, original drawings and prints – along with the most significant of his many churches. Scott was involved with the restoration of almost every Medieval cathedral in England and Wales, but restorations are difficult to represent visually and so illustrations of them concentrate on his splendid new furnishings in a limited number of examples.

Scott was an antiquary as well as an architect. He was also an author, writing several books as well as many reports and lectures and, not least, his *Personal and Professional Recollections*, the first autobiography by an architect to be published (posthumously) in Britain, and extensive quotation has been made from this illuminating text in the pages that follow. Scott combined a romantic vision of the Middle Ages and the architectural expression of a deep Christian faith with a Victorian enthusiasm for progress and invention. His was a Gothic for the steam age.

Gavin Stamp
London
March 2015

PART ONE

GEORGE GILBERT SCOTT

❧ The Fall and Rise of a Reputation

Sir Gilbert Scott was buried in the nave of Westminster Abbey, close to the grave of Sir Charles Barry, on Saturday, 6 April 1878. Scott's funeral was the grandest ever accorded to a British architect, before or since. The only comparison is with that of James Wyatt in 1813, but the government only paid for that ceremony in the Abbey to cover up the fact that King George III's architect was in disgrace, had ruined the Office of Works through his inefficiency and was bankrupt when he died suddenly and violently, leaving his widow destitute. Scott, in contrast, passed away at the age of sixty-six loaded with honours and, having run the largest and most prolific office of its kind in the country, which had covered the land with churches and public buildings, he left a small fortune to his four surviving sons.

Queen Victoria sent an empty carriage to join the funeral cortège of thirty-eight vehicles, which left from the house in South Kensington in which he had died ten days earlier while living there with two of his sons. The coffin was carried through the cloisters of the Abbey flanked by pall-bearers representing the Royal Academy, the Royal Institute of British Architects, and others from among the many professional bodies and institutions with which Scott was associated; while those who joined the procession included the Duke of Westminster and other peers, several bishops, deans and other clergy, and the eighteen staff from his still large but by then somewhat diminished office together with many fellow architects, former pupils and assistants, artists and contractors who had worked with and for him, as well as former clients. The funeral sermon was preached the following day by Arthur Stanley, Dean of Westminster, who spoke of 'the most famous builder of this generation. Others may have soared to loftier flights, or produced special works of more commanding power; but no name within the last thirty years has been so widely impressed on the edifices of Great Britain, past and present, as that of Gilbert Scott.'[1]

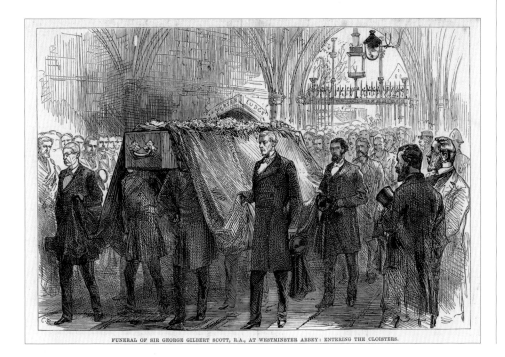

FUNERAL OF SIR GEORGE GILBERT SCOTT, R.A., AT WESTMINSTER ABBEY: ENTERING THE CLOISTERS.

OPPOSITE: The portrait of Scott at the base of the memorial brass over his grave in Westminster Abbey designed by G.E. Street, as copied by Frank Theodore in 1910.

LEFT: The body of Sir Gilbert Scott entering the Cloisters of Westminster Abbey on 6 April 1878, as depicted by the *Illustrated London News*.

Si monumentum requiris... Scott's are many, various and scattered – and almost all in the revived Gothic style he had made his own. The most famous, and conspicuous, 'the result of my highest and most enthusiastic efforts', is the National Memorial to the Prince Consort – the Albert Memorial – in Kensington Palace Gardens. He also built cathedrals, although none is anything like as large and splendid as St Paul's in London, and they are, or were, outside England: in Scotland and in parts of the British Empire overseas, in Newfoundland, South Africa and New Zealand. But some of his more important secular monuments can be found near his last resting place: the Foreign Office in Whitehall, and, a little farther away, the Midland Grand Hotel at St Pancras Station. He was responsible for major public works outside London: in Preston, Leeds and Dundee; he designed new buildings in both ancient English universities and for the universities in Glasgow and Bombay, and for a number of public schools. He designed several large country houses, numerous workhouses and a jail. And the great number of designs for churches – so often with a proud spire, and many accompanied by a vicarage and a village school – which emanated from his busy office are to be found all over the land.

Then there are the church restorations, which constituted a major part of his practice and for which he has received both praise and obloquy. In addition to repairing or improving several hundred Medieval parish churches, Scott worked at almost every ancient cathedral in England and Wales, beginning with Ely in 1847. He was also Surveyor to Westminster Abbey itself, 'a great and lasting source of delight', where one of his achievements was the rescue of the Chapter House from utter degradation. Of this, when writing up the Abbey for the *Buildings of England*, Sir Nikolaus Pevsner added

> *A last word here on Scott and his much attacked restorations. There is one thing at least that ought to be remembered. He found the chapter-house full of bookcases, staircases, galleries . . . If we have any idea to-day of its original noble beauty, Scott has given it us.*

Even so, George Gilbert Scott has had a bad press, and the main reason for this is his controversial restorations of Medieval churches and cathedrals. Today it is possible to appreciate that Scott's restorations were usually scholarly and well judged, but as the leading practitioner in the great campaign to repair long-neglected buildings, to remove what were regarded as inappropriate alterations and bring them back to their original appearance and, at the same time, make them suitable for modern worship in a revived Church of England, he became a scapegoat when educated opinion turned against this practice. Scott felt the slight personally when, in 1874, while he was serving as President of RIBA, John Ruskin declined the institute's Royal Gold Medal (which he himself had been awarded in 1859) as a protest against both restorations and professionalism in architecture. As the critic wrote to Thomas Carlyle, clearly with reference to Scott,

> *I cannot accept medals from people who let themselves out to build Gothic Advertisements for Railroads – Greek Advertisements for firms in the city – and – whatever Lord Palmerston or Mr Gladstone chose to order opposite Whitehall – while they allow every beautiful building in France and Italy to be destroyed, for the 'job' of its restoration.[2]*

By his own account, the news of a restoration by Scott was the catalyst for the founding of 'Anti-Scrape', or the Society for the Protection of Ancient Buildings, by William Morris in 1877. In a preparatory letter published in the *Athenaeum* that year,

The Chapter-house in its present state.

Morris wrote

My eye just now caught the word 'restoration' in the morning papers, and on looking closer, I saw that this time it is nothing less than the Minster of Tewkesbury that is to be destroyed by Sir Gilbert Scott. Is it altogether too late to do something to save it – and whatever else of beautiful and historical is still left to us on the sites of ancient buildings we were once so famous for?

This was unfair, for Scott had been involved with Tewkesbury for over a decade and the restoration work, which had begun in 1874, was comparatively tactful. But Morris was not interested in fairness, for Scott was too conspicuous and convenient a target – later he would describe the architect as 'that (happily) dead dog'. In truth, Scott could not win: as he remarked about his restoration proposals for St Albans Abbey, 'I am in this, as in other works, obliged to face right and left to combat at once two enemies from either hand, the one wanting me to do too much, and the other finding fault with me for doing anything at all.'

What was announced at Tewkesbury in 1877 was a second appeal for funds. In his 1864 report on the Abbey, Scott had proposed 'the removal of disfigurements, such as the modern pews, galleries and whitewash, and the bringing of the interior back to something like a state of propriety and to some approach to its original beauty'.[3] It is easily forgotten what a very bad structural state many Medieval buildings were in by the mid-nineteenth century – well illustrated by the dramatic collapse of the crossing tower and spire of Chichester Cathedral in 1861 – and how crass and damaging many post-Reformation, and especially Georgian, interventions were. What would sometimes be at issue was the subjective matter of what constituted a 'disfigurement', and Scott could undoubtedly be guilty of prejudice against later Classical furnishings. But very often the greatest damage was due to the modernising enthusiasm of the clergy who were in charge

ABOVE LEFT: The interior of the Chapter House before Scott's restoration: woodcut by Jewitt from *Gleanings from Westminster Abbey*, 1861.

ABOVE RIGHT: Scott rediscovered: exposing an original ceiling in the Foreign Office in 1987.

ABOVE: The staircase in the
Midland Grand Hotel at
St Pancras in 1966, then
threatened with demolition.

of sacred buildings – archdeacons and deans, rectors and vicars – who did not always share their architect's reverence for ancient fabrics, and against whom he had to battle, sometimes in vain.

In his many writings on the vexed question of church restoration, Scott was anxious to declare himself a 'Conservative' rather than a 'Destructive' or 'Eclectic' restorer, and modern research has only been able to confirm a handful of cases in which Scott removed genuine Medieval work in favour of a scholarly but hypothetical reconstruction of an earlier phase in the building's history. A lot of the heat in the restoration debate was generated not so much by the actual proposals but by different religious perspectives, and by the question – as pertinent today as in the nineteenth century – as to whether ancient churches were historical monuments or living, and therefore changing, places of worship. As Scott wisely observed, 'It will be useless to endeavour to persuade seriously thinking people that it is wrong "to restore churches from motives of religion". They were built from such motives, and must ever be treated with like aim.'

In the opinion of his former assistant and his future successor as Surveyor to Westminster Abbey, J. T. Micklethwaite, Scott

could restore a design from a few remains with a skill that ensured a very close resemblance to the original work, and that faculty may have tempted him to carry out the work of restoration to a greater degree than modern criticism approves of. On the other hand there are two or three things to be considered. In the first place, the custodians of a building on which Sir Gilbert was employed would not have allowed him to do anything else than restore it in the manner he did, and those restorations he treated as he did would, in all probability, have been done much worse if he had not done them, or if they had been done by men who did not possess his skill.[4]

Three decades after his death, M. S. Briggs argued against the common view that 'Scott and all his followers were nothing better than vandals'. It was, he believed,

fashionable among a large number of architects and others to regard him in this light at the present time, but to what extent these people are informed as to facts is more doubtful. The man who never made a mistake has not hitherto been discovered, and until this happens we must allow for defects in everyone. Without attempting to deny that Scott was guilty of faults more or less grave in the course of his professional career, it must in justice be admitted that if it had not been for his marvellous constructive ingenuity, his painstaking thoroughness, and his profound knowledge of mediaeval architecture, many of our cathedrals would have collapsed, and many more would have been mangled by far less trustworthy hands than his own.[5]

Indeed, because of his fame and ubiquity Scott was sometimes blamed for sins committed by others. In the case of Westminster Abbey, it was the more arrogant and less scholarly J. L. Pearson, not Scott, who, in undoing alterations made to the North

Transept in the early eighteenth century, destroyed and altered the design of the original rose window and the blank tracery in the gable. Scott's achievement here, towards the end of his life, was the recovery of the design of the three great portals after much careful investigation. Another later Surveyor, W. R. Lethaby, the 'Anti-Scrape' disciple of Morris and the SPAB, was prepared to admit that Scott's 'copy' of the original was 'generally "correct"', while regretting the replacement of original stone (see p. 195). With regard to the restoration of the Chapter House, while disagreeing over details, Lethaby was prepared to say that 'Scott almost discovered this wonderful building'.[6] And another of the severest critics of his restorations, the Revd W. J. Loftie, once wrote that this building was 'in great danger of complete downfall. The most determined opponent of "restoration" must approve the greater part of the work carried out by Sir Gilbert Scott in 1865 and subsequent years.'[7] As for St Albans Cathedral, it was Scott's persecutor and 'the leader among those who wish me to do what I ought not to do', the dreadful E. B. Denison, later Sir Edmund Beckett and later still Lord Grimthorpe, who was responsible for vulgarising and partly destroying the ancient Abbey church after Scott was safely out of the way. Among Scott's achievements there was the piecing together from hundreds of buried fragments of marble and stone of the shrine of St Alban – a work that so impressed Ruskin that he even offered to underwrite the cost.

One reason for Scott's general success as a church restorer was that he got on well with bishops and deans. This was partly because of his strong Evangelical Christian background. Devout and sincere, he came from a clerical family, and several of his brothers and other relations were clergymen. His eldest son considered that Scott 'was an *Anglican* essentially & in the best sense of the term. Decidedly opposed to Roman practices on many points, principally on the use of Images . . .' Among Scott's many former assistants, Bodley and Street belonged to the Anglo-Catholic wing of the Church of England, and it tended to be such High Church architects who were responsible for the more original and striking Gothic church designs. Scott, however, belonged firmly to the middle, to the Broad Church; as he famously remarked: 'Amongst Anglican architects, Carpenter and Butterfield were the apostles of the high church school – I, of the multitude.' And it was this desire 'to tread the "*via media*"', combined with his instinct for compromise that partly accounted for his success. The architect Edward M. Barry considered that,

> *Sir Gilbert Scott was neither by taste nor temperament an innovator. In the midst of controversy his works showed sobriety of design, and moderation of judgement. The Tractarian movement and the Gothic revival went, indeed, hand in hand; but he was too earnest a champion to wish his cause to be identified with any single party.*[8]

Like any highly successful man, Scott was criticised in his lifetime – and not just over his church restorations. The suspicion arose early that he did far too much, and that he must surely have needed to delegate much of his design work to assistants. For Scott was running what must have been by far the largest architectural office in Britain, if not in Europe. At the height of Scott's fame and activity in the 1860s, there were some thirty-six assistants, pupils and other staff working for him in the house in Spring Gardens, just off Trafalgar Square, which he had used as his office since 1838. After Scott's death, *The Builder* published a list of 732 buildings attributed to him; the following year, in a letter to G. G. Scott junior, his former assistant Charles R. Baker King compiled a list of 541 works which had emanated from the office, acknowledging that it was far from complete as workhouses, schools and parsonages were not enumerated. A century later, Scott's biographer David Cole listed 879 jobs. Such industry naturally attracted comment, not necessarily favourable.

A well-aimed attack came from the Scottish architect Alexander 'Greek' Thomson, dismayed that the huge job of designing the new buildings for the university in Glasgow had been given to a London architect who practised, as far as that brilliant Classical designer was concerned, in an alien, barbarous Anglo-Saxon style. In his public lecture delivered in 1866, 'An inquiry into the appropriateness of the Gothic style for the proposed buildings for the University of Glasgow, with some remarks on Mr Scott's plans', Thomson made some remarks which, breaking that pathetic convention that architects do not criticise each other's work, mercilessly dissected the design of the proposed new building and added pertinent observations about its architect's method of business.

> . . . granting that Mr Scott is all that his most enthusiastic admirers would have him to be, everybody knows that his establishment being the most fashionable in the great metropolis, his business is so enormous that, to expect him to bestow more than the most casual consideration upon the work which passes through his office, is altogether unreasonable . . . Nor could it be supposed that the magnitude of this work was sufficient to have secured more than an ordinary amount of attention at his hands, for it was nothing unusual to him.[9]

In fact, this was an opinion about Scott already confirmed by the university's own agent in London, who reported back that 'perhaps you are not aware of his enormous occupation & of the common report that it is physically impossible that he can give personal superintendence to much that he undertakes'. But more important was what 'they had heard of the eminent talent & taste of Mr George Gilbert Scott of London' and his office's reputation for efficiency, speed and for being able to produce architecture of high quality.[10] He was appointed without competition, and the university was certainly not disappointed with the Gothic pile that rapidly rose in a few years on top of Gilmorehill.

Stories circulated concerning Scott's presumed lack of knowledge about what was done in his name. Much repeated since, some were recorded by his former assistant, Sir Thomas Graham Jackson, almost half a century later.

> There are many amusing tales which show the slight acquaintance he had with what came out of his office: how he admired a new church from the railway carriage window and was told it was one of his own; how he went into a church in process of building, sent for the clerk of works, and began finding fault with this and with that till the man said, 'You know, Mr Scott, this is not your church; this is Mr Street's, your church is farther down the road'.[11]

Other anecdotes were recalled by Lethaby:

> It is told that once, having left town by the six o'clock train, 'the office', on slackly assembling, found a telegram from a Midland station asking, 'Why am I here?'. On another journey he is said to have noticed a church that was being built and to have inquired who was the architect – 'Sir Gilbert Scott'. These are doubtless fictions, but tales tell.[12]

(Are such stories told of our knighted and ennobled 'starchitects' today? If not, why not?)

A view expressed at the time, and often since, was that Scott was a follower rather than a leader, a facile designer who was more interested in success than in creating original works of art. In his *History of the Gothic Revival* published in 1872, a comprehensive

summary of what had been achieved over the preceding century, the architect and future
Keeper of the National Gallery, Charles Locke Eastlake, wrote that Scott

> *must be accredited with the power of keeping pace with the steadily advancing ability*
> *of his contemporaries. It has been said of Mr Scott's later work that it does not rise*
> *above the level of popular appreciation. To this he would probably reply that those*
> *examples of architectural design which exhibit greater originality are the productions*
> *of men who in many instances differ entirely from each other as to the principles of*
> *beauty in their art, and that while such works have been exposed to severe criticism,*
> *his own have escaped direct censure.*[13]

Some contemporaries were rather harder on Scott. One was the architectural critic and
historian James Fergusson who, in the second edition of his *History of the Modern Styles
of Architecture* published in 1873, objected to the 'incongruous mediaevalism' of Scott's
work at St Pancras, in contrast to the 'plainness' of King's Cross Station next door (so
anticipating the later modernist prejudice in favour of the supposed rational modernity
of the Great Northern Railway's terminus, and against the apparent archaism of the better
planned and better built Midland Railway terminus). 'There is no proportion between
the shed and its uses,' Fergusson argued, 'and everything looks out of place, and most of
all the Gothic mouldings and brickwork, borrowed from the domestic architecture of
the Middle Ages, which with its pretty littlenesses thrusts itself between the gigantic iron
ribs of the roof.'[14]

Another enemy was J. T. Emmett, a mediocre architect but a ferocious critic, who,
in an anonymous article in a literary journal in 1872, attacked the insensitivity and
commercialisation of the Gothic Revival in general and Scott's work in particular.
Emmett ridiculed '"eminent persons" in the profession' and, surely with Scott in mind,
asserted that 'there are ludicrous but authenticated tales of their ignorance of their own
nominal works'. At St Pancras, he wrote, there was

*a complete travesty of noble associations, and not the slightest care to save these
from sordid contact; an elaboration that might be suitable for a Chapter-house, or
a Cathedral choir, is used as an 'advertising medium' for bagmen's bedrooms and
the costly discomforts of a terminus hotel; and the architect is thus a mere expensive
rival of the company's head cook in catering for the low enjoyments of the travelling
crowd.*[15]

Emmett also had a go at Scott's cathedral work, suggesting that, 'the reredos at Ely,
and the screens at Lichfield and Hereford, are sufficient monumental records of the
audacity of an architect and of the simplicity of his employers'.[16]

Like so many successful architects then as now, Scott was acutely sensitive to criticism
to the point of paranoia. He took any adverse comments personally and invariably
responded to them at length in print. As regards the Midland Grand Hotel, he confessed,

*This work has been spoken of by one of the revilers of my profession with abject
contempt. I have to set off against this, the too excessive praise of it which I receive
from other quarters. It is often spoken of to me as the finest building in London; my
own belief is that it is possibly* too good *for its purpose.*

This was a confession that recognised that the great elaboration of the hotel was not
in accord with the principle of 'propriety' in architecture advanced by Scott's hero and
mentor, Augustus Pugin. T. G. Jackson later recorded that his old employer seemed to

have taken a dislike to him about this time, and learned that 'he was under the impression that I was the author of a very slashing article in the *Quarterly Review* which made havoc of him and the school to which he belonged'.[17]

Emmett's attack came at a difficult time for Scott: 1872 may have been the year he had the honour of being knighted by the Queen following the completion of the structure of the Albert Memorial, but it was also the year his wife Caroline died, inducing in her grief-stricken husband an outpouring of emotion and guilt about his neglect of her and his family. Success had come at a cost. He was not well; his health had been in decline since he was taken dangerously ill at Chester in 1870, and he was beginning to wind down his practice. It was also at this time that the missionary zeal of the Gothic Revival was abating, and a younger generation of architects – including not only many of Scott's former assistants but also his own architect sons – were beginning to question the very ideals of the movement of which Scott was widely regarded as a leader, and they were experimenting with other styles of architecture (one of Scott's very last pieces of writing was a criticism of the new 'Queen Anne' style).

When Scott died six years later, the tributes were many and sincere. *The Times* devoted a leading article to his career, observing that, 'There are few parts of England where his name is not familiarly known and where memorials of his art and genius are not to be found.' Contemporary opinion held that Scott was 'the foremost architect of his day' and, in its obituary, *The Builder* described his as 'the most successful architectural career of modern times'. Perhaps a more balanced judgement came from E. W. Godwin, Whistler's architect, who wrote that he

> should hesitate to nominate Scott's work as those of a genius. If he had not the great gift he however possessed others which in these days are perhaps even more conducive to success. He was indefatigable in business and a fervent worker. No chance was ever missed, no opportunity neglected.[18]

And this was the opinion of Scott that generally prevailed for the following century: that his success and fame came more from industry than from great architectural ability.

Scott's first biographer was the architect and writer Martin Shaw Briggs, who published a series of articles on his life and work in the *Architectural Review* in 1908. 'In the annals of nineteenth-century architecture,' he began, 'the name of Sir Gilbert Scott occupies a foremost place, a place which was won by his remarkable talents, his sterling character, and his unflagging tenacity of purpose.' The drawback, he found, in writing his 'sketch' was the fact that Scott's practice 'was not only the largest but also the most fraught with historical and national importance that has fallen to the lot of any architect since the Great Fire'. Although the Gothic Revival was then still flourishing (not least in the hands of Scott's grandson, the future Sir Giles Gilbert Scott), even in the Edwardian period, before the Great War, there had long been a reaction against what is today termed High Victorian Gothic, which now seemed coarse and lacking in refinement. Briggs could still admire Scott's churches – he thought the Episcopalian cathedral in Edinburgh 'undoubtedly one of the most beautiful of all Scott's designs, and shows him at his best' – but he could not stomach the secular Gothic buildings which, to modern eyes perhaps, may seem the more interesting and original. The offices in Broad Sanctuary next to Westminster Abbey, 'an opportunity of displaying his ideas of "Domestic Gothic" . . . serves to show us the fallacy of supposing that plate-glass, sash-windows, mullions, and tracery can ever live at peace together'. As for Walton Hall, it was 'a house exhibiting the very lowest depths of Victorian Gothic'.[19]

Kenneth Clark devoted a chapter to Scott in his pioneering study of the Gothic Revival published in 1928 and concluded that,

He was, indeed, a man of great talents, but these were not specifically architectural, were, rather, Gladstonian, and would have won him a high place in public life. Of these talents the chief, and the first to bring him fame, was industry.[20]

But such was the general contemporary ignorance about the Victorians that Clark was happy to repeat the absurd canard that the St Pancras Station hotel was simply the rejected Gothic design for the Foreign Office, adapted to a different site and function. Writing a few years later about Early Victorian architecture, the architect and historian Albert Richardson concurred:

On the whole his work was neither admirable nor thoughtful; it lacked genuine grace; its feeling was brittle and hard . . . That he was an architect of more than average ability cannot be denied, but he was not a great artist.[21]

During much of the first half of the twentieth century and beyond, when Victorian architecture was generally despised and ridiculed, Scott was held to be representative of his time.

For Pugin led to Gilbert Scott, and Scott created the Albert Memorial, and beyond the Albert Memorial lay the wastelands of Victorian and Builder's Gothic, where all the sentimental bad taste of a nation converged on public and domestic creations the horrors of which only time and war have laid waste.

This was the conventional, unthinking opinion of one historian writing in 1952.[22] Reginald Turnor, in his study of *Nineteenth Century Architecture in Britain* published two years earlier, noted that, 'Nowadays the Albert Memorial is treated as London's chief architectural joke' (something it had perhaps been since Lytton Strachey subtly ridiculed it in his life of Queen Victoria) and his verdict on Scott was that his

self-assurance was, on the surface at least, colossal; his instinct for combining financial success with a rather smug morality seems to be of the very essence of his time; his enormous output of bad and indifferent architecture reflects that Victorian philistinism which sprang out of the moralisation of art.[23]

Scott's works were not, however, usually as much vilified as were the more distinctive and original creations of William Butterfield; they were rather dismissed as conventional, pedestrian. 'Will anyone ever admire the works of Scott?' wondered the Revd Basil Clarke in 1938 in his pioneering study of Victorian church architects: 'It is hard to believe that they will, for there is nothing in particular in them to admire.'[24] Even John Betjeman, despite his growing enthusiasm for Victorian architecture, considered at first that 'chief Gothic stylist, Sir Gilbert Scott, was a man who, for all the 700 and more buildings that he designed, produced comparatively few which were original'.[25]

This consistently dismissive attitude towards Scott was well expressed by the architect and historian H. S. Goodhart-Rendel, and as that most wise of critics was an influential pioneer in the re-evaluation of Victorian architecture, his opinion still deserves some respect, and therefore repeating.

That the architect who, during a working career of forty years, built or interfered with nearly five hundred churches, thirty-nine cathedrals and minsters, twenty-five universities and colleges, and many other buildings beside, was a remarkable man it would be foolish to deny. That the designs he issued, the making of which must, considering their number, have been in more or less degree deputed to others, should mostly possess a strong flavour of their issuer's idiosyncrasy is as remarkable as it might be unexpected. That that idiosyncrasy, however, was compounded of any qualities more valuable aesthetically than prudence, industry, and a strong sympathy with the popular taste of the moment, cannot be easily maintained. Throughout the first forty years of Queen Victoria's reign, large buildings of Scott's constantly check the historian's progress, some of them deserving more admiration, some less. None, however, is likely to justify in our eyes the judgement of an age that throned him upon an eminence relatively loftier than that occupied by any other British architect since the day of Sir Christopher Wren.[26]

By the 1950s, however, with major Victorian buildings beginning to come under threat, attitudes began to change – a process culminating in the foundation in 1958 of the Victorian Society. Notoriously, the new society first encountered defeat in the battle over the Euston 'Arch', but the next two major engagements that it had to fight were both to defend important buildings by George Gilbert Scott – and both, ultimately, ended in victory. These battles encouraged a reappraisal of his achievement. The first concerned the product of the long saga involving Scott and Lord Palmerston following the most farcical of all nineteenth-century architectural competitions, the Foreign Office in Whitehall, whose replacement was announced by the government in 1963. In its argument against demolition, the 'Vic Soc' quoted the historian Christopher Hussey:

'For a century the spectacular Italianate pile, thanks to Palmerston's inspired obstinacy, has played the visual role intended by Inigo Jones to be filled by Whitehall Palace in the centre of the historic square mile comprising Westminster and St James's. Seen from the park down the lake, the dramatic mass of black and white Portland stone enriched with countless statues composes . . . one of the most grandly picturesque urban landscapes in the world.'[27]

The eventual reprieve of the building and the restoration and adaptation of its interior revealed reception rooms as splendid and distinctive as any of their time, and confirmed that Scott was as adept in the Classical manner in which he had been trained as he was in the Gothic he had made his own (see p. 151).

The second battle was over St Pancras Station. Scott's hotel there, the Midland Grand, had been seriously threatened with demolition in the 1930s, but survived in office use. In 1966, however, British Railways announced that both St Pancras and its neighbour would be replaced by a new station. Quite what this involved was never made explicit, and there was respect for both the apparent rationality of King's Cross Station and Barlow's stupendous train shed at St Pancras, but what was absolutely clear was that Scott's great railway hotel, now unloved, neglected and spoiled internally, was to go (see pp. 14 & 17).

LEFT: A page from the travel diary kept by Scott on his tour of France in 1862.

FAR LEFT: Some pages from the notebooks in which Scott wrote down his Recollections.

The society fought back, and Betjeman did his best to change public opinion. He tried to enlist the help of his old friend John Summerson, the fastidious historian of Georgian London, who, at first, declined.

> *No. I just couldn't put any heart into the idea of preserving it . . . Every time I look at the building I'm consumed with admiration in the cleverness of the detail and every time I leave it I wonder why as a whole it is so nauseating . . . I shall hate to see all that gorgeous detail being hacked down but I really don't think one could go to a Minister and say this is a great piece of architecture, a great national monument.*[28]

But then, significantly, Summerson changed his mind and the following year wrote what was introduced as a 'cool appraisal' of the arguments over St Pancras for the *Illustrated London News*. Recalling when the building was still a hotel, he began by commenting on changing attitudes:

> *We forget how deeply Victorian things – especially Victorian buildings – were hated in those days. St Pancras Hotel, in particular, was loathed for its size and pretension, its colour and ornamentation, and I think also for the obviously rather improper association of cathedral architecture with railway lines; for railways in those days were railways, not dear quaint old things . . . Today, with St Pancras Station and hotel in danger of dispersal and possibly demolition, a somewhat different attitude prevails. St Pancras, to a new generation, is glorious, unique, romantic, its skyline sheer poetry, its detail exquisite. St Pancras must be saved.*[29]

It was – largely thanks to Nikolaus Pevsner and the Victorian Society, assisted by Lord Kennet (Wayland Young) who, as Parliamentary Secretary to the Ministry of Housing and Local Government, upgraded the listing of the station from III to I. And nothing so well illustrates the revival of interest in things Victorian, and the change in the reputation of Sir Gilbert Scott, than the eventual triumphant restoration of both the train shed and the former hotel in the early twenty-first century, which was greeted with enthusiastic public acclaim. Happily, the reopening of Scott's building in 2011 as the St Pancras London Renaissance Hotel, superbly restored, complete with a smart restaurant named after the architect, coincided with the bicentenary of his birth. This concluded the full rehabilitation of Scott's reputation; Simon Jenkins reported how *the St Pancras hotel finally reopened to defy the forces of darkness. It is restored to its old magnificence . . . The finest booking hall in Europe clinks with cocktails. The murals on the old staircase throb with colour. Arches leap across corridors and gilt drips from vaulting. Victorian restaurants, bedrooms and bars are booked solid. Sometimes, just sometimes, beauty wins.*[30]

And Simon Heffer, in a positive new general history of the Victorian age, can write that 'Scott was one of the period's greatest architects, and one of its greatest egos'.[31]

Other examples of Scott's extensive legacy also exercised the Victorian Society in its early years. Two of his screens were removed from cathedrals he had restored. At Salisbury, in 1959, a zealous dean began to emulate Wyatt 'the Destroyer' by removing the metal and timber screen as well as Scott's reredos and the Victorian stained glass in the Chapter House. At Hereford, the screen was Scott's most spectacular, created with Francis Skidmore in cast and wrought iron, timber, brass, copper, semi-precious stones and mosaic. It had been shown at the 1862 International Exhibition in London (see pp. 18 & 196), when it was described by the *Illustrated London News* as 'the grandest most triumphant achievement of modern architectural art . . . far the most important and successful example of modern metalwork that has been executed'. In 1966 it fell victim to anti-Victorian prejudice but, fortunately, was not destroyed. After being in store, in pieces, for some years, it ended up at the Victoria and Albert Museum in 1983 and, after a careful and challenging restoration, has been shown in pride of place in the metalwork gallery since 2001. At Salisbury, Pevsner had commented that the destruction of Scott's work was 'a crime against the tenets of the Victorian Society, but the need of the C13 cathedral was indeed greater than theirs'. But by 1974 he could write of Scott's screen in Lichfield that it was

of the highest craftsmanship and an ornament to any cathedral. Let Salisbury and Hereford be vandals and remove their Scott-Skidmore screens, Lichfield must hold out till High Victorianism is at last fully appreciated in its best work.[32]

Happily, Lichfield held out.

In 1977, Scott's 'best' church, All Souls, Haley Hill, was closed and abandoned, declared redundant two years later. Its stonework was alarmingly decayed owing to a problem its architect did not anticipate: a catalytic reaction between the limestone and sandstone he had used. All Souls seemed doomed. But SAVE Britain's Heritage commissioned a scheme for its repair, and in 1981 the Friends of All Souls was formed to save the church. Eventually, thanks to financial aid from the National Heritage Memorial Fund, the Historic Buildings Council and other charities, organisations and individuals, Scott's masterpiece was reroofed and its spire strengthened. In 1989 it was vested in the Redundant Churches Fund, now the Churches Conservation Trust, and today the restoration continues (see p. 125).

The slow process of rehabilitating Scott eventually resulted in the careful restoration of the much-abused Albert Memorial. In the 1980s, Mrs Thatcher's Conservative government had declined to fund the repair of that national monument and by 1993, concealed by scaffolding and awnings, it was on English Heritage's 'at risk' register. Auberon Waugh suspected a conspiracy

to deprive us of one of London's best-loved monuments. Among those born in the first half of the dreadful decade of the 1930s, it is still considered clever to despise the achievements of the nineteenth century – intellectually, scientifically and artistically the most exciting century in the history of the world.[33]

However, thanks to a campaign led by the Victorian Society, the Memorial was carefully restored, and in 1998, with Scott's 'realisation in an actual edifice, of the architectural designs furnished by the metal work shrines of the middle ages' now colourful and glittering again, and with John Foley's seated figure of her great-great grandfather re-gilded, it was rededicated by HM the Queen Elizabeth II (see p. 21).

The centenary of Scott's death in 1978 had been marked by a memorial service in Westminster Abbey, at which Scott's successor as Surveyor, Stephen Dykes Bower, observed that,

> *Burial in Westminster Abbey is an honour that sets a certain seal on the reputation of those few to whom it is accorded. In that respect it might seem self-sufficient. But in rare cases discernment prompts something more: commemoration of an event or anniversary that has come to have a new significance of which we should be reminded . . . The sum of his achievements is what now has recognition: in view of past depreciation recognition that constitutes an act of reparation.*[34]

Today that reparation is almost complete, and it is possible to make a fair and balanced assessment of Scott's achievements. There can be no doubt that he, or rather his practice, did far too much. It seems unlikely that Scott was personally responsible in detail for every design that emanated from his office in Spring Gardens, although, as Goodhart-Rendel admitted, that office – full of talent as it was – did produce work in a consistent, recognisable style. Many of the buildings attributed to Gilbert Scott are indeed pedestrian, and sometimes disappointingly mediocre. But it is clear that when Scott bothered, when he took a keen interest in a project, he could be very good indeed.

Scott deserves to be judged by the buildings that were the product of his enthusiastic and close attention. These must include the Albert Memorial, the Foreign Office and the Midland Grand at St Pancras. He was also personally involved in the cathedral restorations and refurnishings, as the investigation of Medieval fabric was something that deeply interested him. And some of those many – too many – churches are the thoughtful products of his own hand. This was usually the case with the estate churches designed for rich and aristocratic clients, such as those at Nocton, Sherbourne and Ranmore Common. There is the splendid All Souls, Haley Hill, outside Halifax, built for the local industrialist and MP, which is so representative of the aspirations of the 1850s, and which its architect proudly considered 'on the whole, my best church'. Then there is the magnificent tall church he built in Hamburg but that is, alas, now a ruin.

Scott was not an innovator in terms of the development of Gothic, although he showed great resourcefulness in combining new materials and technologies with Medieval precedents in his major secular buildings – something he advocated in his influential book, *Remarks on Secular & Domestic Architecture, Present & Future*. Scott lacked the inventive brilliance of Butterfield; nor was his work ever as intriguingly eccentric – or simply vulgar and exhibitionistic – as that of, say, S. S. Teulon or E. Bassett Keeling. But although the more extreme examples of Victorian Gothic have long delighted 'Vic Soc' aficionados, good architecture is not necessarily original. Nor should it be: too much architectural history has concentrated on the innovative rather than on the accomplished – and the beautiful. To form a fair assessment of Scott's architecture, it is worth recalling Betjeman's later opinion of it. 'For the last ninety years almost,' he wrote in 1972,

> *Sir Gilbert Scott has had a bad press. He is condemned as facile, smart, aggressive, complacent and commercial. When at the top of his form Scott was as good as the*

ABOVE LEFT: Scott's sketch, made in August 1827, of the chapel at Gawcott, Buckinghamshire, which his father had just rebuilt.

ABOVE RIGHT: The interior of the Mediaeval parish church of All Saints at Hillesden, Buckinghamshire, as drawn by the young Scott on 22 January 1826.

best of his Gothic contemporaries . . . I used to think that Scott was a rather dull architect, but the more I have looked at his work the more I have seen his merits.[35]

Many of his numerous buildings are well worth looking at closely.

What is surely remarkable is that, while running a busy practice and being personally involved in the design of many of the practice's buildings, Scott found the time to write (and he wrote well and lucidly) and to edit several books – not least his *Remarks on Secular & Domestic Architecture*, a major contribution to the developing philosophy of the Gothic Revival. This was because he was so often on the move and 'pretty well all that I write is the product of my travelling hours'. Scott made very productive use of those interminable hours spent in railway carriages rushing around Britain for site visits, to meet clients or to address restoration committees; indeed, his immensely productive career would have been impossible without the extensive and efficient Victorian railway system (along with the electric telegraph and a most efficient and quick postal service).

Furthermore, in addition to preparing lengthy reports on the condition of cathedrals, Scott wrote and delivered many public lectures on architecture and restoration practice, including a series of inspirational lectures at the Royal Academy of Arts on the rise and development of Medieval architecture (which frequently provoked applause from the student audience). These, posthumously published, reveal Scott to have been a serious antiquary and scholar, as does his earlier book, *Gleanings from Westminster Abbey*. His knowledge of Medieval architecture and sculpture was profound, and his love of it genuine and passionate. He delighted in the detailed investigation of ancient buildings, and had great powers of observation. This is confirmed by the diary he kept on one of his many Continental tours (the only one to survive the destruction of most of his personal papers).

During the 1840s and 1850s, Scott visited Germany, Bohemia, Austria, Italy and France, assiduously sketching all the while. In the autumn of 1862 Scott made another tour of France. His particular purpose was to study the early Byzantine-Romanesque churches of Périgord and Burgundy – Angoulême and Périgeux, for example – so as to make a design for the Royal Albert Hall in a 'round-arch byzantine' style. Acquiring drawings of domes, arches, capitals and other useful details at these buildings was something that a busy architect could have delegated to an assistant, but Scott clearly wanted to see them for himself. And his responses to them are not those of a hard-nosed and ambitious practitioner who merely managed a busy office churning out designs, for he delighted in what he saw. At Auxerre, he thought the doorways

> *a most remarkable assemblage of art, & deserve long and careful study. If the sculpture had been* antique *we should have casts of it in all our museums, but being mediaeval it is allowed to perish as it may. But oh – protect it from restoration!!*

At Vézelay, he found that

> *the great feature . . . is the sculpture. It is* perfectly *marvellous not however for beauty but for the* Violence *of the archaism. I never saw anything more extraordinary.*

And at Périgeux, he closely inspected 'Poor St Front!', then being ruthlessly restored by Paul Abadie (Scott, like most English architects, considered French restorations to be more wholesale and thus much worse than those they were conducting in England). After taking 'some pains to ascertain the extent of [the] authenticity' of the new work, he concluded that:

> *Internally I have no doubt the restoration is authentic but why so absolute a renewal?! The old domes* were *once of rubble groyns filled in on a boarded centering – the marks of the boards are still visible as in our Norman staircases.*

This travel diary is also revealing about Scott's character and energy. He covered some 1,300 miles, largely by railway, in just over three weeks, travelling alone and, presumably, light. Nor did he arrange to be treated as a distinguished foreign visitor, although he was by then the architect of the Foreign Office in London, and famous. When, a decade earlier, he had encountered Eugène Viollet-le-Duc sketching in Westminster Abbey, he had given the Frenchman letters of introduction to travel elsewhere in England. But Scott did not attempt to have the compliment returned (possibly because he was not happy with Viollet-le-Duc's approach to restoration), which left him at a disadvantage when he visited the Abbey at St Denis.

> *. . . my object was to study the north portal of the Transept. I found however a determined opposition to my admission not one step towards facilitating w^h would the officials take not even to the extent of telling me where the clerk of the w^k could be found. I made a sketch of it from the street by the help of my glass . . . I then returned to my post opposite the transept & fortunately observed that the men in leaving for dinner did not lock the gates so when the coast was clear I slipped in and in haste & fear picked up a scanty crop of details. The doorway though truly excellent is simple – the pedestals only moulded. The capitals are admirable some of the very best Byzantinesque carving I have ever seen.*[36]

Sadly, Scott's assiduousness was in vain, at least as regards the Albert Hall, for none of his several designs for it – both Byzantine and Gothic – found favour with the South Kensington authorities.

Although there are numerous published studies of individual buildings by Scott – including two books about the Foreign Office saga – there is, as yet, no major comprehensive monograph on Scott similar to those devoted to other great Victorians such as

Burges and Norman Shaw. The literature on Scott remains comparatively modest, given the scale of his reputation and achievement. After M. S. Briggs contributed his series of four articles on Scott's life and work to the *Architectural Review* in 1908, and Kenneth Clark's chapter on Scott, there was a long interval before the architect David Cole published an admirable study of Scott's life and work in 1980, complete with a list of works. After studying Scott's work for many years, Ian Toplis had nearly completed a biography when he died in 2010. The problem, no doubt, has been the sheer size of Scott's achievement which has daunted historians. But the scale of Scott's oeuvre is not, unfortunately, matched by commensurate associated archival material. Following his death, Scott's second son, John Oldrid Scott – who inherited the office – disposed of most of the drawings as well as personal papers, including correspondence between his parents. As he wrote in justification to J. T. Irvine, 'the quantity was so enormous that it was quite necessary to thin them down'.

Fortunately we have Scott's *Personal and Professional Recollections*, one of the first autobiographies of a British architect – indeed, of any architect – to be published. This book has been the principal source for almost all that has been subsequently written about him. While Scott's text can seem at once innocently naive and self-regarding, and has often been used against him, the factual accuracy of his own account of his life and achievements has not been seriously questioned. Scott began writing down his recollections in 1864, at first 'primarily for my children', but he clearly thought in terms of publication soon afterwards and in 1873 made precise instructions about the reproduction of the manuscript after his death; no doubt conscious that he might be accused of vanity in doing this, he explained that

I feel it due to myself that the statement of my professional life should go before the public in a fair and unprejudiced form; and the more so as I have been one of the leading actors in the greatest architectural movement which has occurred since the Classic renaissance.

Scott wrote his recollections in pencil in a series of five leather-bound notebooks. Like his lectures and cathedral reports, they were scribbled down while the architect was on the move (see p. 23).

Recollections was published posthumously in 1879, having been edited by his scholarly architect eldest son, George Gilbert Scott junior. The names of some of Scott's adversaries – particularly during the Government Offices affair – were tactfully omitted by the editor, who also cut many long and painful passages concerning the deaths of his third son, Albert, and his wife, Caroline. However, some of this material was retained for publication, and evidently surprised and shocked some readers. The reviewer in *The Architect* complained of 'indiscretions' included by the editor and in the Introduction contributed by the Dean of Chichester, John Burgon.

'It was not his business,' writes Thackeray of Macaulay, 'to bring his family before the theatre footlights, and call for bouquets from the gallery as he wept over them,' but, as it now appears, the volume before us is suggestive perpetually of posturing of this kind. Nothing is too private for publication.

But it was, in fact. Much was excised but, fortunately, the original manuscript survived and the edited-out material was published almost exactly a century later.[37]

Although the *Morning Post* thought that 'this is one of the most delightful books that has appeared for years', some reviewers were clearly surprised that a modern architect should ever have written an autobiography intended for publication. An editorial in *The Builder* – doubtless the work of its long-standing editor, George Godwin – announced that 'It is rather a bold thing, considering human nature for what it is, that any man should offer his own description of his life and work as the only fair and unprejudiced one', and he went on to complain of

BELOW: The new Fishmongers' Hall designed by Henry Roberts: engraving of c.1837–38 after a drawing by R. Garland.

The frieze has labels including: SCOTT, VANBRUGH, WREN(?), PALLADIO, PUGIN, COCKERELL, BARRY, CHAMBERS, JONES, THORPE

The entire want of recognition of those who were of any service to him . . . there is not one word of recognition of the help he received from some journals when he most wanted it – help which he urgently entreated in letters penned as if his professional life or death depended upon an editor's good-will. And we cannot help feeling that there is something a little undignified in the frequent imputations of malice and reviling, and other strong words, in reference to criticism which in the main was probably as honest as criticism, as the world goes, usually is.

Scott's acute and aggrieved sensitivity to criticism, seemingly common among architects in any age, was confirmed by A. J. Beresford Hope, who wrote how 'he was often hurt in his feelings by things which he could afford to laugh at'. But Hope went on to record that 'with all his zeal, all his earnestness, and all his conviction, he never bore malice. He would take blows, and would give blows, as every man ought to do; but I repeat – he never bore malice.'[38]

Scott certainly thought he had many enemies. 'A race of detractors of me and my work has since arisen,' he complained, 'the mildest of whom say that I have fallen off since my defeat by Lord Palmerston.' In fact, he had very few on a personal level. After his death, many commented on the sweetness of Scott's character, his kindness and generosity – it emerged that he had continued to try and assist his unfortunate former partner long after the dissolution of the firm of Scott & Moffatt. Scott seems to have been regarded with affection and respect by most of his assistants and pupils (with the possible exception of J. J. Stevenson), and the character that emerges from the pages of *Recollections* is an engaging and sympathetic one: a man driven by a strong sense of duty and a deep Christian faith, a man seriously committed to his art, and a loving husband, devoted to his family, as well as a workaholic, acutely conscious of his social and professional status.

What also comes across is Scott's naivety. Like many architects (and, indeed, architectural historians) Scott lived and moved in his own rather narrow architectural world. A good example of this is his record of meeting Arthur Schopenhauer, 'an old German philosopher', in Frankfurt and describing him as 'a determined infidel . . . I meant to have sent him some books on the evidences, &c., of Christianity, but I forgot it'. As the editorial in *The Builder* commented:

> *He was not below the usual standard of the profession in regard to matters of general intellectual interest, but his views and observations upon important subjects beyond the profession are disappointing. It is impossible not to smile at his account of his pleasure in talking to 'an old German philosopher named Schopenhauer', who, however, was apparently an 'Atheist', without apparently the slightest suspicion that he is speaking of a man who fills a much more important place in modern intellectual Europe than Scott or any other modern architect.*[39]

A distinctive aspect of Scott's character that is evident in the pages of *Recollections* is a combination of sensitivity and bumptiousness, and quotations indicating an engaging lack of self-awareness have sometimes been used to make him seem ridiculous. Scott was certainly never shy of proclaiming his own merits. He could write that St Giles, Camberwell, was 'the best church by far which had then been erected'; of the Martyrs' Memorial in Oxford that, 'I fancy the cross itself was better than any one but Pugin would then have produced'; of his rebuilding of Doncaster parish church that, 'I . . . believe it

BELOW: Scott & Moffatt's first, competition-winning design for St Giles' Church, Camberwell: lithograph of 1841.

THE NEW CHURCH OF ST. NICHOLAS AT HAMBURG.

to stand very high amongst the works of the revival'. The Midland Grand at St Pancras was, of course, 'possibly *too good* for its purpose', and as regards his unexecuted design submitted in the competition for the new Law Courts in the Strand: 'Of its parts, I am bold to say, that many exceeded in merit anything that I know of among modern designs.' As for his unexecuted design for the new Hamburg Rathaus, 'I confess that I think it would have been a very noble structure', while of his abortive Gothic design for the Government Offices in Whitehall, he was sure that 'it would have been a noble structure; and the set of drawings was, perhaps, the best ever sent in to a competition, or nearly so'. Perhaps it was. In fact, every one of these claims might now be seen to be true. George Gilbert Scott was a great Victorian, a man of prodigious energy and many talents, who literally created much of the fabric of Victorian Britain; he was also a very good architect.

OPPOSITE: Scott's competition-winning design for the St Nikolaikirche in Hamburg: woodcut from the *Illustrated London News*, 1845.

⚜ 'Virtuous Man, Skilful Architect'

George Gilbert Scott was born on 13 July 1811 at the little village of Gawcott in Buckinghamshire, where his father, the Revd Thomas Scott, was Perpetual Curate and, as an amateur architect, had designed the simple chapel there (see p. 26). Scott's mother was Euphemia Lynch, who had been born in Antigua and was connected with the Gilbert family of planters in the West Indies. In his *Recollections*, Scott was anxious to emphasise that his mother was 'well-born, of a good old family', and that both parents were 'what may be called "well-bred", both by nature and training "gentlefolk"' – something which slightly undermined his intention to show how far he had travelled from his comparatively humble origins to professional success.

Much of the first chapter of *Recollections* was taken up with describing the quaint old rural customs that still then continued in that remote part of the county, a few miles from Buckingham and the great house at Stowe ('really a very fine place'), where he grew up. Scott also emphasised how socially isolated his family was in Gawcott. This was partly because the local clergy ostracised them owing to their Evangelicalism and sympathy for Methodism – his 'aunt Gilbert' had once been kissed by John Wesley, 'which she esteemed a great privilege'. Scott's grandfather was the celebrated 'Commentator', the Revd Thomas Scott, Rector of Aston Sandford in the same county, and the author of *The Force of Truth* and the *Commentary on the Whole Bible*. (Much later, in 1880, when George Gilbert Scott junior was contemplating becoming a Roman Catholic, Cardinal Newman was pleased to see him not least because he was the great-grandson of the 'Commentator', 'the writer who made a deeper impression on my mind than any other, and to whom (humanly speaking) I almost owe my soul'.)

Scott was the third of his parents' thirteen children. He seems to have had a solitary childhood and an unsatisfactory education. 'I ought certainly have gone to school, but this was out of the question. My father was poor, and as he took pupils himself, he was too busy with the older ones . . . to give me much of his personal attention.' In a passage reminiscent of the childhood of another famous architect, Edwin Lutyens, Scott recorded that 'I had very little companionship, and I became a solitary wanderer in woods and fields, and about the old churches, &c., in the neighbourhood'. Reading between the lines of *Recollections*, it seems that Scott was a late developer and a difficult youth, which may have been because he was jealous of his more academically successful brothers. He admitted that his eldest brother, Thomas, had 'remarkable talent and was viewed as a little god by his brothers and even by his parents. This had a bad effect on

LEFT: Scott's competition-winning but unexecuted design for the Hamburg Rathaus: watercolour perspective, possibly by J. D. Wyatt, c.1854.

me.' All but one of Scott's five surviving brothers, both older and younger, went up to the University of Cambridge, and were ordained priests, and it may well be that resentment and consciousness of his failings was the driving force behind his later furious ambition. 'How infinitely important it is for boys to feel the duty and necessity for exertion,' he later admitted. 'Though I have reason to be most thankful for my success in life, the defects of my education have been like a millstone about my neck, and have made me almost dread superior society.'

By the age of fourteen, Scott must have been a problem to his family, but, because of his interest in the old churches in the locality (especially that at Hillesden) and his aptitude for sketching (encouraged by the drawing-master, Mr Jones of Buckingham), his father thought he might become an architect. Scott was therefore sent off to stay at nearby Latimers with his uncle, the Revd Samuel King, for about a year where he was taught mathematics and the rudiments of architecture. Scott's father and uncle then had to find an architect to whom the boy could be articled. 'It was a *sine-quâ-non* that he should be a religious man, and it was necessary that his terms should be moderate.' Their choice fell on James Edmeston of London, an Evangelical and a poet who, today, is better known as a hymn writer – 'Lead us, Heavenly Father, lead us / O'er the world's tempestuous sea' – than as an architect. For Scott it was initially a disillusioning experience:

> *I went to him with a mythic veneration for his supposed skill and for his imaginary works . . . The morning after I was deposited at his house, he invited me to walk out and see some of his works – when – oh, horrors! The bubble burst, and the fond dream of my youthful imagination was realized in the form of a few second-rate brick houses, with cemented porticoes of two ungainly columns each!*

Edmeston's dim practice then largely consisted of building villas in Hackney and occasionally designing a school. Worse, he had no time for Gothic, as he found it expensive to build. When his new earnest and romantic pupil designed farm buildings 'in true rustic style', he 'wrote seriously to my father, warning him that I was employing my leisure hours on matters which could never by any possibility be of any practical use to me'. Scott did, however, acknowledge that he learned a great deal about the practical and business side of architecture during his time with Edmeston, and made good use of his architectural library. He also, for a short while, attended lessons given by the architectural drawing-master George Maddox, whose skill he recognised but whom he found 'far from being an estimable man in other ways. He was an infidel and his conversation on such subjects was truly appalling.' A further consequence of Scott's four years in his office was that there he met another pupil who would become his future professional partner, William Bonython Moffatt (1812–87), the son of a builder and 'a remarkably intelligent, though uneducated boy, a native of Cornwall'.

In 1831, having completed his articles and obtained an introduction to Samuel Morton Peto (a fellow student at Maddox's), Scott gained further valuable experience by working for a time with the contractors Grissell and Peto, who were then building the new Hungerford Market, one of London's most remarkable lost buildings (Charing Cross Station now stands on the site) (see p. 28). Designed by Charles Fowler, it was a sort of shopping centre, on two floors, stretching from the Strand down to the Thames, where there were two partly iron-framed taverns.[40] Scott was stationed there and learned much from the fact that

> *The work was constructed on principles then new. Iron girders, Yorkshire landings, roofs and platforms of tiles in cement, and columns of granite being its leading*

elements . . . I ought, too, to mention the advantage of constant reference to Mr Fowler's working drawings, some of the best and most perspicuous I have ever seen.

The following year, as it 'became necessary that I should be doing something for my living', Scott became an assistant to the architect Henry Roberts, another Evangelical and one with a strong social conscience. He had recently won the competition for the Fishmongers' Hall, that splendid Greek Ionic palace at the north-west corner of the new London Bridge, (see p. 29) and Scott

(see p. 29)

had the advantage of making all the working drawings of this considerable public building, from the foundations to the finish; and of helping in measuring up the extras and omissions, as well as of constantly seeing the work during its progress.

While working for Roberts, Scott attended one of the last series of lectures at the Royal Academy given by the aged Sir John Soane. Later, in 1834, Roberts appointed Scott clerk of works for the building of the Camberwell Collegiate School, a feeble brick Gothic building, long since demolished.[41]

Having been with Roberts for two years, Scott was now anxious to set up in practice on his own, and he was soon able to do so owing to one of the most heartless pieces of legislation ever enacted by a British parliament. The period of Scott's pupillage was a time of social unrest and political turmoil, culminating in the passing of the Great Reform Bill in 1832. Two years later, in the year the old Palace of Westminster burned, the Poor Law Amendment Act was passed by the Whig government. This abolished the previous system by which the responsibility for the relief of the indigent and unemployed fell on parishes; the burden of relief was now transferred to boards of guardians representing a 'union' of parishes, and no able-bodied man was to receive assistance unless he entered a workhouse. These buildings, in the words of Edwin Chadwick, the friend of Jeremy Bentham and the chief Poor Law Commissioner who inspired the Act, were to be 'uninviting places of social restraint'. The workhouses built by the new unions were, in consequence, usually prison-like buildings planned on utilitarian or Benthamite principles with a radiating 'panopticon' plan, and were most effectively satirised by Pugin in his illustrations of 'Contrasted Residences for the Poor' published in the second edition of his notorious *Contrasts* of 1841.

Many new workhouses were needed, and quickly. The man charged with producing model plans for them was Sampson Kempthorne, who owed his position as official architect to the Poor Law Commissioners to nepotism. As he was young and inexperienced, Kempthorne invited his friend Scott to move into the vacant rooms next to his own in Carlton Chambers in Lower Regent Street at the end of 1834, to assist him with the designs. This arrangement lasted only a few weeks before the death of Scott's father, in February 1835, changed everything and he realised he 'must adopt my course with promptitude, or my chances in life were gone'. Necessity galvanised him into action; he wrote 'a kind of circular to every influential friend of my father's I could think of, informing them that I had commenced practice, and begging their patronage'. The result was that Scott was entrusted with the design of a number of workhouses in Buckinghamshire, Northamptonshire and elsewhere. What followed was

an era of turmoil, of violent activity and exertion. For weeks I almost lived on horseback, canvassing newly formed unions. Then alternated periods of close, hard work in my little office at Carlton Chambers, with coach journeys, chiefly by night, followed by meetings of guardians, searching out of materials, and hurrying from union to union, often riding across unknown bits of country.

To cope with the work, Scott employed a clerk and, in the summer of 1836, invited Moffatt, his former colleague in Edmeston's office, to help him with making drawings and supervising works. As Moffatt was already architect to the Amesbury Union workhouse in Wiltshire, the two architects soon agreed to collaborate as equals, eventually becoming the architectural partnership of Scott and Moffatt. Scott designed some workhouses on his own, notably in Northamptonshire and Lincolnshire, but on the whole the two architects worked together, with Moffatt usually securing the commissions, which were open to competition. Scott acknowledged his partner's talent for 'union hunting':

Moffatt's own exertions were almost superhuman, and when I recollect that no railways came to his help, I feel perfectly amazed to think of what he effected . . . The competitions for union workhouses were conducted on principles quite peculiar to themselves . . . On the day on which the designs were to be examined the competitors were usually waiting in the ante-room, and were called in one by one to give personal explanations, and the decision was often announced then and there to the assembled candidates. Moffatt was most successful in this kind of fighting, having an instinctive perception of which men to aim at pleasing, and of how to meet their views and to address himself successfully to their particular temperaments. The pains he took in improving the arrangements were enormous, communicating constantly with the most experienced governors of workhouses, and gathering ideas wherever he went. He was always on the move . . . He was the best arranger of a plan, the hardest worker, and the best hand at advocating the merits of what he had to propose, I ever met with; and I think that he thoroughly deserved his success, though it naturally won him a host of enemies and traducers.

Scott was also on the move for much of the time – just as he would be later in his career, after the rapid construction of a national network of railways in the 1840s made travel much easier.

I lived, like Moffatt, in a constant turmoil, though less so than he. The way in which we used to rush to the Post Office, or to the Angel at Islington, at the last moment, to send off designs and working drawings, or to set off for our nocturnal journeys, was most exciting, and one wonders, in these self-indulgent days, how we could stand the travelling all night outside coaches in the depth of winter and in all weathers. The life we led was certainly as arduous and exciting as anything one can fancy in work, which in its own nature was so dull as our business in the abstract was, but one's mind seems to shape itself to its day, and I believe I really enjoyed the labour and turmoil in which I spent my time. These were the last days of the integrity of the old coaching system, and splendid was its dying perfection! It was a merry thing to leave the Post Office yard on the box-seat of a mail, and drive out amidst the mob of porters, passengers, and gazers.

In all, Scott and Moffatt were responsible for over forty workhouses. 'Dirty disagreeable work,' Scott later admitted, 'but the rule should be never to pick your subjects but go in for whatever offers whether you like it or not, for if you compete only for the subjects you like you will nearly always fail.'[42] Their success was partly due to their 'improved plan' which,

instead of a square or radial arrangement, offered three distinct structures: an entrance range (often lower in height), a T-shaped main building with the accommodation for the master and matron in the centre, separating the accommodation for males and females, and, at the rear, an infirmary flanked by workshops. Many of these structures were grimly utilitarian if vestigially Classical, but some of the later workhouses – Amersham, Belper, Billericay, Dunmow, Macclesfield, Mere and Windsor – were given a Tudor Gothic or Jacobean treatment, often with patterned and diapered brickwork in several colours, and these were among the most expensive of all New Poor Law workhouses.[43]

Scott and Moffatt also secured commissions for two other important institutions which brought the practice to public attention. One was the Infant Orphans Asylum (today a courthouse) at Wanstead in Essex, won in competition, where the plan was Moffatt's and the Jacobean treatment of the elevations Scott's. Prince Albert laid the foundation stone in 1841, and the building was opened by Queen Victoria's uncle, Leopold, King of the Belgians, two years later. The other was the Berkshire County Gaol at Reading, a design in the castellated castle manner thought appropriate for such structures, completed in 1844. Here the practice ran into difficulties over the estimates, and the building – in which, notoriously, Oscar Wilde would be incarcerated at the end of the century – eventually cost as much as eight of those hated 'Bastilles' for the poor, the workhouses.

By 1838 Scott was doing well enough to marry his second cousin, Caroline Oldrid, to whom he had been engaged for three years and had known for a decade. She was already his sister-in-law, as Scott's elder brother Thomas had married her sister Fanny, while Scott's sister Euphemia married Caroline's brother Henry. In his *Recollections*, Scott rather typically noted that the mother of his 'dearest Carry' was the daughter of William Scott of Grimblethorpe Hall in Lincolnshire, the brother of the Commentator, but he did not mention the fact that her father, 'Mr Oldrid of Boston', was in trade: he was a draper, and there is still a shop carrying his name in Boston today. The honeymoon was a tour via Southwell and Matlock to Malvern and Bristol, returning via Oxford. Soon afterwards they moved to a brick Georgian terraced house just south of Trafalgar Square, 20 Spring Gardens (renumbered 31 in 1866) where they lived above the office (Moffatt continued to work from his house in Kennington). Their first child, George Gilbert Scott junior, was born there in 1839.

Scott was now in a position to pursue his enthusiasm for the Gothic, which had been frustrated for some years. He resumed sketching Medieval churches and began to design new ones. The first was a 'poor barn' in the Early English style, faced in flint and red brick, designed for his uncle King at Flaunden in Hertfordshire. This was followed by a church at Lincoln – St Nicholas – won in competition and designed in a mean Early English Gothic; Scott was later ashamed of it and could not

say anything in its favour, excepting that it was better than many then erected. Church architecture was then perhaps at its lowest level . . . Unfortunately everything I did at that time fell into the wholesale form; and before I had time to discover the defects of my first design, its general form and radical errors were repeated in no less than six other churches.

The great Victorian church-building boom, the material expression of the revival of the Church of England, was then beginning, but these first efforts are not impressive. That at Norbiton near Kingston is an effort in the most unfortunate and ungainly of architectural styles, the Neo-Norman. The best is the new church at Hanwell: Early English, with what would become a typical Scott steeple with a broach spire, visible from Isambard Kingdom Brunel's great viaduct taking the Great Western Railway across the River Brent built just a couple of years earlier.

The defects Scott became conscious of were the 'contemptible character of their fittings', the 'use of plaster for internal mouldings, even for the pillars', but above all, the absence of a proper chancel, 'my grave idea being that this feature was obsolete'. In the Evangelical tradition of Christianity with which Scott was most familiar, a long chancel as in a Medieval church was indeed an anachronism, but Scott was now becoming aware of a new agenda for church design which was being set by two powerful influences. The first was the Cambridge Camden Society, the pressure group founded by undergraduates at the University of Cambridge in 1839 under the influence of the Oxford or Tractarian Movement in the established Church. Its members sought to revive ancient Catholic liturgy and practices and, to that end, to restore or recreate Medieval church planning and arrangements. Scott made contact with one of the founders of the society, Benjamin Webb, because he was exercised about the proposed destruction of the gutted but restorable remains of St Stephen's Chapel, the former House of Commons, in the Palace of Westminster ('The destruction of this precious architectural relic is the single blot on the fair shield of Sir Charles Barry'). When they eventually met, 'Mr Webb took advantage of the occasion to lecture me on church architecture in general, on the necessity of chancels, &c., &c. I at once saw that he was right, and became a reader of the "Ecclesiologist".' He was elected a member of the society in 1842.

Although his churchmanship was far removed from the Anglo-

Catholicism of the Camdenians, Scott was clearly anxious to keep in with the new society as soon as, via its journal *The Ecclesiologist*, it came to wield much power. The designs for new churches which failed to follow the principles its editors laid down (which were really Pugin's principles) were roundly criticised and in 1843 lists of 'Architects Condemned' and 'Architects Approved' were published. Scott naturally sought approval and, for a while, enjoyed it. But then, as he typically complained at length in *Recollections*, they became 'my most determined opponents. My subsequent success was, for many years, in spite of every effort on their part to put me down by criticisms of the most galling character.' The reason, he supposed, was

> that I was not thought a sufficiently high churchman, and as they fell in at the same time with my very excellent friends Carpenter and Butterfield, they naturally enough took them under their wing. This no one could complain of: but the attempt to elevate them, by the systematic depreciation of another equally zealous labourer in the same vineyard, was anything but honourable . . . To expose the misdoings of ignorance and vandalism was their duty; to point out the shortcomings of their fellow-labourers would have been a kindness; but to treat friends and allies with studied scorn and contumely, through a series of years, because they had not sworn implicit allegiance to their absolute régime, was discreditable to the sacred cause which they professed to make the object of their endeavours.

Another reason was that Scott later accepted the commission to design a church in Germany for the Lutherans. In the end, the society's intolerance and bigotry went too far and, in 1845, it had to be dissolved and refounded in London as the Ecclesiological Society.

The second influence was, of course, that of the great Pugin. In *Recollections*, Scott described the effect of reading his books as a sort of Damascene conversion. 'Pugin's articles excited me almost to fury, and I suddenly found myself like a person awakened from a long feverish dream, which had rendered him unconscious of what was going on about him.' Scott read the articles which appeared in the *Dublin Review* in 1841, and which were later republished as *The Present State of Ecclesiastical Architecture in England*, and he presumably also read *The True Principles of Pointed or Christian Architecture* which appeared the same year. Scott was not just influenced by Pugin's ideas, for many of his early churches are very closely modelled, in both plan and style, on those built and illustrated by his hero. It is recorded that Scott visited Pugin's celebrated church at Cheadle shortly before it opened in 1846, the Earl of Shrewsbury writing to its creator that, 'He admired everything *exceedingly*. The stencilling absolutely made the water run down both sides of his mouth.'[44]

'Being thus morally awakened, my physical dreams followed the subject of my waking thoughts. I used fondly to dream of making Pugin's acquaintance.' But when he did Scott was slightly disappointed, for, 'He was tremendously jolly, and showed almost too much *bonhomie* to accord with my romantic expectations. I very rarely saw him again.' But it says much for Scott that he remained devoted to Pugin's memory. A quarter of a century later, when he was famous and successful, Scott was anxious to honour his late hero by including him in John Birnie Philip's sculptural frieze on the Albert Memorial (see p. 30). When the Queen insisted that Scott himself should be represented there, he wrote to her equerry that

> I have . . . chosen an unobtrusive position behind the figure of Pugin to whom I desired to do all honour as the head of the revival of mediaeval architecture and in many respects the greatest genius in architectural art which our age has produced . . .

OPPOSITE: The Palazzo della Ragione, formerly the Town Hall, at Verona as sketched by Scott on his first visit to Italy in 1851 and showing his skill as a draughtsman.

He was our leader and our most able pioneer in every branch of architectural work and decorative art . . . My ambition, then, would be to appear as his disciple, and to do him all the honour he deserves and which there is a strong feeling to deny him.[45]

Now he was awakening, Scott had an opportunity to show what he could do in the correct Gothic line when, in 1840, he won the limited competition for the Martyrs' Memorial in Oxford. His design was based on the surviving Eleanor crosses and today makes an illuminating contrast with the adjacent and exactly contemporary Ashmolean Museum and Taylorean Institute, that late and most sophisticated expression of Neo-Classicism in England by C. R. Cockerell. 'I fancy the cross itself was better than any one but Pugin would then have produced,' Scott later claimed. But he was naive: the memorial was proposed by Protestant Anglicans as a deliberate counter to the growing influence of the Tractarian movement in the university – Pugin violently objected to its erection, not because of the design but because it commemorated the wrong sort of martyr, Protestant rather than Catholic. Scott was similarly naive – or opportunistic – a few years later when he agreed to design an Anglican church in Ramsgate which was to be built in opposition to the threat seemingly posed in the town by the Roman Catholic church of St Augustine which Pugin had built next to his own house, The Grange. Christ Church in Vale Square is a good church, if derivative, but it is curious that, as Pugin's modern biographer remarks, 'it came about that the church in Ramsgate which most directly reflects Pugin's influence was built in a deliberate attempt to counter it . . . More tellingly, it was Scott who was building the Puginian church while Pugin himself had moved on.'[46]

Scott's opportunity to show that he had learned lessons came with the first of two opportune fires. The old parish church of Camberwell in south London burned in 1841 and there was a competition for a new church on the site. With Edward Blore as assessor, it was won by Scott and Moffatt with a design in Decorated Gothic with a west steeple, transepts and a short apsidal chancel (see p. 31). But this was not what was built and consecrated in 1844. Local opposition forced Scott to make a less costly design, which now had a prominent tower and spire over the crossing and a generous square-ended chancel. 'My conversion to the exclusive use of real material came to its climax during the progress of this work, and much which was at first shown as plaster was afterwards converted into stone.' St Giles, Camberwell, remains one of Scott's finest churches, as good as anything Pugin had yet achieved and yet with a robust character of its own. Even *The Ecclesiologist* considered it 'one of the finest ecclesiastical structures of modern days' while, inevitably, finding fault with many of its details and with the fact that it had galleries.

The other conflagration was abroad. In 1842 the first great fire of Hamburg destroyed most of the port, and two years later Scott was made aware of a competition for the rebuilding of the city's cathedral, the Nikolaikirche.

Strange to say, I had not then seen anything of continental architecture, except during part of two days which I had spent at Calais. I at once, however, made up my mind that the style of the design must be German gothic, and that I must without delay make this my study. I accordingly set out on my first continental tour . . .

. . . visiting Cologne, Frankfurt, Marburg and elsewhere. Scott made his first sketch designs on the boat back from Hamburg before a stormy crossing and seasickness put him out of action for several days. Time was short to meet the competition deadline. As Scott acknowledged, the drawings were prepared largely by his new assistant, George

Edmund Street, together with Henry Coe. They were sent off by steamer but arrived three weeks late owing to the early icing up of the Elbe; they were, however, accepted.

Scott's account of this competition was somewhat disingenuous. The project to rebuild the Nikolaikirche – a Lutheran church – was mired in heated controversy: the questions of style and of church planning were affected by the politics of religion between Protestant and Catholic, and was fuelled by growing German nationalist feeling. And the idea that Gothic was German was encouraged by the momentous project, commenced in 1842, to complete the west front and towers of Cologne Cathedral. In Hamburg, there was a desire at first to retain and restore the damaged steeple of the old church, and Gottfried Semper, the rising star of German architecture, based in Dresden but a native of Altona across the river from Hamburg, prepared a design for incorporating this with a new Gothic building. Once the decision had been made to demolish the old church completely and hold a competition, Semper prepared a design for a centrally planned domed church in a Romanesque-Byzantine style. Later, to be on the safe side, he also made a design in Gothic. In all, thirty-nine architects submitted forty-four designs to the competition.

Scott and his local agent seem to have been well aware of the nationalist sentiment in favour of Gothic.

> When my drawings arrived and were exhibited with the rest, the effect upon the public mind in Hamburg was perfectly electrical. They had never seen Gothic architecture carried out in a new design with anything like the old spirit, and as they were labouring under the old error that Gothic was the German ('Alt Deutsch') style, their feelings of patriotism were stirred up in a wonderful manner. My design was to their apprehension far more German than those of any of the German architects.

Nevertheless, the lay assessors placed his scheme third and that by Semper first (a fact not recorded in *Recollections*). However, there was strong and organised local opposition to Semper's design, which was dismissed as 'un-German'. Scott lobbied hard, and suggested that the committee seek the advice 'of some eminent antiquarian'. Eventually, Sulpiz Boisserée and Ernst Zwirner were approached and, as the former was the driving force behind the Cologne Cathedral project and the latter (who made the final decision) its architect, their advice was a foregone conclusion: Scott, despite being a foreigner, got the job. It has to be said that his behaviour was devious at times – at one point meeting Zwirner and members of the jury in Lübeck as if by accident – and that Semper was shabbily treated, leaving him aggrieved and threatening litigation.[47]

The foundation stone of the new Nikolaikirche was laid in 1846 and it was consecrated in 1863, the original design having been enhanced with high transepts; the magnificent west tower and spire – for a while the highest in Europe at 147 metres – was completed in 1874. For the historian Edward Freeman, an important influence on the Gothic Revival, the design was 'the noblest work that three ages have produced, the pile whose lofty spire would seem to call adoring crowds to the Church's most gorgeous worship'.[48] With its verticality, dramatic modelling with flying buttresses and pinnacles, it was certainly one of Scott's finest and most impressive churches but, sadly, it was badly damaged in 1943 when British bombs created the murderous firestorm that devastated the centre of Hamburg. Most of what was left was demolished in 1951, leaving only the steeple standing as a landmark and as a forlorn monument to Anglo-German architectural collaboration. Scott spent much time in Germany in 1845 and 1846, and became friends with another important figure in the German Gothic Revival, August Reichensperger (who owned a great Gothic chair designed by Scott).[49] Later, in 1855, largely thanks to Reichensperger,

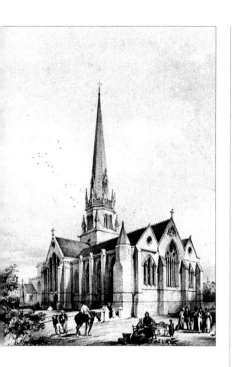

ABOVE: Scott's design for restoring St Mary's Church in Stafford, showing a new spire which was not built as well as a rebuilt south transept.

OPPOSITE: The frontispiece, drawn by A.W.N. Pugin, of *Views of the Church of St. Mary at Stafford* by the late John Masfen, jun., published in 1852.

Scott won the competition for a new Rathaus in Hamburg with a Gothic design based on the Cloth Hall at Ypres, but this came to nothing (see p. 34).

At home, Scott's success in Hamburg was criticised, almost predictably, in the pages of *The Ecclesiologist*. With ineffable condescension and piety, the anonymous author, while 'bound to confess that the spire is beautiful, and well managed', condemned Scott for designing a building

> *for the worship of one of the worst sections of an heretical sect . . . how must we characterise the spirit that prostitutes Christian architecture to such a use? . . . We do earnestly trust that Mr Scott's example will not be followed. We are sure that the temporal gain of such a contract are a miserable substitute indeed for its unrealness, and – we must say it – its sin.*[50]

But Scott did not repent, and, in what would become his usual fashion, he responded at length and gave as good as he got, with cogent arguments both theological and architectural. He pointed out that the position of the Lutheran Church was, theologically, similar to that of the Church of England, that Luther had views on symbolism in church architecture which were very sympathetic, and that Pugin himself had stated that 'he could, when first entering an ancient Lutheran church, hardly perceive that it was in the hands of Protestants', and that 'it is to churches which are "occupied by the Lutherans" that we must look for examples of the movable fittings of mediaeval churches'. This letter, written in July 1845, *The Ecclesiologist* did not deign to publish but 'gave a worse than garbled statement of it'.[51]

By this time, the partnership of Scott and Moffatt was coming under strain as the paths of the two architects, very different in temperament, had diverged while the practice was not making money. In *Recollections*, Scott wrote that a

> *constantly increasing desire had grown up in my mind to terminate the partnership … My wife was most anxious upon the subject, and was constantly pressing it upon my attention, but my courage failed me, and I could not muster pluck enough to broach it. At length Mrs Scott 'took the bull by the horns.' She drove to the office while I was out of town, asked to see Mr Moffatt privately, and told him that I had made up my mind to dissolve our partnership. He was tremendously astounded, but behaved well, and the ice thus broken, I followed up the matter vigorously.*

This passage has often been used against Scott, implying that he was either cowardly or devious and that he dumped Moffatt once he ceased to be useful to him. The original manuscript of *Recollections* reveals that this was not in fact the case. After the partners won the commission for Wanstead Asylum, Scott thought that 'Moffatt's head was turned! He used to boast that he could *afford* to make a fool of himself. His talent and energy remained, but he was an altered man. He cared not who he offended either by dissent annoyance or indirectly by his strange way of conducting himself.' By 1845, Moffatt had

> *got into a sad way of offending employers. This grew rapidly upon him till it became* most serious *and I was formally and seriously warned of its consequences. He was also extravagant, keeping four horses, and one thing with another all our practice led rather to debt than to laying by money. Besides this, the great Railway speculation mania was just then coming on and Moffatt was severely bitten, so much so as to be*

absolutely wild, and the line of practice he was actually getting into partook so much of a speculative character as to be decidedly dangerous.

So Mrs Scott acted not a moment too soon, before the growing bubble of Railway Mania burst early in 1846, ruining many investors and precipitating an economic depression. By the end of 1845 it was agreed that the partnership was dissolved, but the official announcement of this was not made until after a year of transition had passed.

The difficulties with Moffatt are also suggested by the diary of Charles Matthew Strange, his assistant in 1859–60, who recorded that he was 'an ugly man with hair all over his head', and how, on one occasion, 'Mr M. not been to bed all night, sparring with some fellows at the George and Blue Boar'.[52] But Scott acknowledged what he owed to his former partner.

He was very talented, very practical, and very industrious. Nor am I sure, with all its drawbacks, that I have not gained more than I have lost by the connexion. My natural disposition was so quiet and retiring, that I doubt if I should have alone pushed my way. My father used to be seriously uneasy on this head, and he never believed that I could get on in the rough world. Mr Moffatt supplied just the stuff I was wanting in. He was thoroughly fitted to cope with the world.

At least for a while. Moffatt went on to design the Earlswood Asylum in Surrey and the Shire Hall at Taunton, but in 1860 he was arrested for debt and was incarcerated for six months in the Queen's Bench Prison before being released after application for *habeas corpus*. Scott contributed twenty pounds towards his legal fees, and it is likely that he continued to help his former partner. Following Scott's death, Moffatt wrote to *The Times* claiming credit for, among other buildings, the Nikolaikirche in Hamburg – a claim immediately and authoritatively refuted by G. E. Street, who had worked on the project himself. 'Moffatt's misfortunes in subsequent years have been a great sorrow to me,' Scott wrote in his *Recollections* in 1864.

They have been the natural consequence of speculative practice and indeed of speculation wholly alien to his profession. He never recovered the moral damage of that year of Speculation Mania 1846, and I can never cease to be thankful that I escaped in time. I was 35 years old in the midst of my year of transition . . . From this time my life seems to have usually run so smooth a course that I hardly know what to say about it that is worth saying.

From this date, Scott's practice indeed ran a smooth course, becoming larger and larger. As he had moved his family to St John's Wood in 1844, the Spring Gardens house could now be taken over entirely by the expanding office. Two men crucial to the running of it had come to Scott and Moffatt in 1841: John Burlison, who became an indispensable 'head man', and John Drayton Wyatt, who became chief draughtsman. Scott had also begun taking pupils. One was Street, who at the memorial meeting held at the RIBA after Scott's death recorded that: 'I can say truly that his extreme kindness and amiability to the young men in the office were such to impress them very deeply.'

Another early pupil who would go on to great things was G. F. Bodley, who arrived in the year of transition and served a long, old-fashioned apprenticeship of five years, living with Scott and his wife at their home in Avenue Road. He was in fact related to Scott, as his sister Georgina had married Scott's younger brother, Samuel King, a doctor in Brighton.[53] 'I had not drawn at all before,' Bodley later recalled. 'The only sketch I remember making was one of the sea at Brighton when the moon made a broad path of light that led to mystery and darkness. I remember showing it to Scott, who said it was not architecture – which it certainly was not.' Bodley found his early work in the office 'rather dreary', as he later confessed to Edward Warren. 'He did not take kindly to the dry and academic expositions of Classic architecture, and of the "Orders", which he met with at first, but his enthusiasm revived with employment upon drawings for Gothic buildings.'[54]

Perhaps it is surprising that, despite his awakening to Gothic, Scott was still giving his pupils the sort of education he had received in Edmeston's office two decades earlier. (This did not continue: when T. G. Jackson arrived at the office in 1858, 'The five orders of classic architecture were scoffed at. We were never made as pupils to draw them.'[55])

At first, after setting up in practice on his own, Scott needed work to survive. He later recalled how

> *My wife was ever an admirable helper to me in my business, always ready with wise advice and encouragement. At one time, after my separation from Mr Moffatt, we were for some years in straitened circumstances, but she always encouraged me to face them out boldly, and by God's blessing they gradually mended till at length we became very prosperous.*

The necessary work soon came in. Thanks to the recovery of the economy after the 'Hungry Forties' and the contemporary revitalisation of the Church of England, combined with the growing enthusiasm for Gothic architecture, there came a seemingly endless stream of commissions for new churches and the restoration of old ones. As his obituarist in *The Builder* magazine wrote:

> *The secret of the success of Scott's career was, that he, partly from inherent talent, partly from the fortunate circumstance of entering on his professional life on the flood-tide of the new spirit in architecture, was the man able above all others to take advantage of that tide, to turn it fully to account, and to sail into prosperity on its current.*[56]

By 1855, David Cole concluded, new jobs were arriving at the rate of one a fortnight and that, after two decades of unremitting toil, Scott was under considerable strain. But he had chosen his lieutenants well, and the office was already very well organised, with Wyatt and Burlison dashing around the country on the new railways keeping everything under control. About one job in Dorset Scott wrote to his client that year, 'Mr Wyatt knows the particulars more correctly than I do,' and to another, 'Mr Burlison is abroad' (probably in Hamburg).[57]

Scott soon became known primarily as a church architect. Many of his new churches were at first very Puginian in their style, usually Decorated Gothic, and plain, often with an asymmetrically sited steeple. Good examples include St Peter's, South Croydon; St Matthew's, Westminster; and the church built for the workers of the Great Western Railway at Swindon. Scott went on to develop a distinct style of his own, however, which relied more on vigorous surface modelling and much carving and figure sculpture. The representative example must be his 'best', the church of All Souls at Haley Hill outside Halifax. It was built in 1856–59 by the local industrialist and MP, Edward Akroyd, who also created 'Akroydon', the adjacent workers' village initially designed by Scott (and continued

RIGHT: The interior of St John's Church in Leeds before the first restoration of 1866–68.

by his former pupil W. H. Crossland). All Souls is conspicuous for its picturesque massing, with a prominent north-west steeple on a sloping site, and was notable for magnificent stained glass by Hardman and Clayton and Bell, and the extensive use of figure sculpture by John Birnie Philip, which *The Ecclesiologist* considered to 'open a new era of church art'. Scott had 'shown once more that he has no superior in vigorous handling of the pure national ecclesiastical style . . . From the richness and correctness of its arrangements it deserves to be reckoned among the most remarkable churches of the revival.' But Scott himself thought that 'it labours under this disadvantage, that it was never meant to be so fine a work as it is, and consequently was not commenced on a sufficiently bold and comprehensive plan'.

One important and difficult job Scott owed to yet another fire. The old parish church of St George in Doncaster burned in 1853 and Scott was commissioned to design its replacement, having found what remained of the old church beyond restoration (see p. 39). Changes were made to the size and scale of the building to secure more accommodation, but the principal difference between the old and new churches is in style. Scott retained the general proportions of the burned church and was anxious to reproduce the old crossing tower, 'a noble work in early and bold perpendicular'. The problem was that, according to the orthodoxy established by the Cambridge Camden Society, Perpendicular was 'debased', and the best phase of Gothic was held to be the Decorated. So St George's was designed in Geometrical Decorated, including the tower. 'I am not proud of this tower. I missed the old outline, and I never see it without disappointment.' For the first time, Scott had here to endure the bullying interference of 'my friend, and at the time my tormentor, Mr E. B. Denison', who became Sir Edmund Beckett and then Lord Grimthorpe, the lawyer and amateur architect who was the son of the local MP and promoter of the Great Northern Railway, whose locomotive works had been sited in the town.

Scott himself advocated this stylistic orthodoxy. To 'best promote the successful revival of Christian architecture', it was necessary to start with what was recognised as the best period of Gothic architecture, 'to adopt in our new works (for the present, at least) exclusively that variety which may be considered the highest development yet attained'. And for Scott, it was what he termed 'the "Geometrical" variety of the "Middle Pointed"' (he had never liked Rickman's terminology: 'EE', 'Dec.' and 'Perp.') which combined 'the grandeur of the "Early English"' with 'the elegance of the flowing style' which was the ideal style for adoption. 'Its great merit . . . consists in its *completeness*.' But Scott was not so blinkered as to dismiss entirely the later Gothic, the Perpendicular, although he thought that 'it contains at every stage some element of decay'.

Nearly all writers on Gothic architecture seem to delight in vilifying its later stages. To myself, I confess, it would be impossible to speak of the naves of Winchester and Canterbury, the choirs of York and Gloucester, the mighty hall of Westminster, or its miniature imitation at Eltham, the roofs and screens of Somerset, otherwise than in terms of deep respect and admiration.[58]

In the 1850s, some of Scott's churches reflected the fashions for French and Italian Gothic. This involved the breakdown of the orthodoxy that 'The revived style was one, and its unity was "Middle Pointed".' This fashion, he thought, followed the abortive Lille Cathedral competition of 1855–56 (won by two Englishmen, Burges and Clutton) and that, 'Its most ludicrous feature was, the pious devotion to "First Pointed" in its most ultra-Gallic form.' As for himself, in 1864 Scott described how he 'gradually fell into the use of French detail, not exclusively, but in combination with English'. He sometimes followed the French use of the square rather than round abacus – the top layer of a column capital – and noted how his client at Bradfield, the Revd Thomas Stevens, 'got to employ the term "square abacus" as a moral adjective, used in the sense of manly, straight-forward, real, honest, and all cognate epithets'. It was a style 'I, on the whole, most delight in'. Later, Scott was 'inclined to think that, even relinquishing the Gallic mania . . . a legitimate style may be generated by its union with later developments'. A good example of a French influence (though with round abacuses) is the church at Shirley near Croydon (in the churchyard of which Ruskin's parents are buried). Here the exterior walls are of flint and stone, there is mild polychromy in the interior, the piers are simple and round and there are some quirky details. At Ranmore Common near Dorking in Surrey, an estate church, there is an unusual octagonal steeple rising above a vaulted crossing, bold naturalistic carving and walls of contrasting ashlar and rough pebbles.

Scott had travelled in France for the first time in 1847 when he studied Amiens Cathedral and the Sainte Chapelle in Paris. 'My eyes were at once opened. What I had always conceived to be German architecture I now found to be French.' Perhaps the most French of Scott's creations was the chapel he designed for Exeter College, Oxford in the mid-1850s to replace a seventeenth-century building. The new chapel, tall, heavily buttressed and, with its apsidal east end, clearly inspired by the Sainte Chapelle, dominates the quadrangle of the college. It is vaulted in stone and enhanced by windows by Clayton and Bell. Eastlake wrote that: 'Although this stately building exhibits here and there, especially in its decorative details, evidence that its designer was not uninfluenced by the now rapidly-increasing taste for Continental Gothic there is nothing in the design which suggests a thorough conversion to the new doctrines.' And the interior was 'most impressive by reason of its elegant proportions, the refinement of its detail, and the sumptuous nature of its embellishments'. A modern historian concludes that, 'Nowhere in Oxford has the spirit of romantic mediaevalism been more compellingly conveyed.'[59] Scott used a similar design, though broader in proportion, for the expensive new chapel for St John's College, Cambridge, but with the addition of a tower modelled on that at Pershore Abbey.

Scott crossed the Alps for the first time in 1851 when he took a 'short tour' in Italy with his friend, the architect and Pugin's future biographer, Benjamin Ferrey. By this time, the writings of John Ruskin in particular were directing English architects towards the colourful Gothic of Italy. The two travelled through Germany to Vienna, then to Trieste and by water across to Venice, where 'all was enchantment! No three days of my life afford me such rich archaeological and art recollections.' There he encountered Ruskin and 'spent a most delightful evening with him'. Scott travelled as far south as Florence and Siena, visiting many other cities en route. But this was not a holiday: every available moment was spent in sketching the details of the exotic buildings he was seeing for the first time (see p. 40). The two 'worked as hard as men could do from morning to night.

We usually breakfasted by twilight, to get every hour of the day for hard work.' Scott recalled in 1864 that 'I gained very much by this journey, and much desire to repeat it. I was convinced, however, that Italian Gothic, as such, must not be used in England, but I was equally convinced, and am still, that the study of it is necessary to the perfecting of our revival.' The fruits of that study would soon be seen in his work, but more in the secular field than the ecclesiastical.

On the whole, as an expert obituarist observed, Scott's architecture had

> the merit of being a thoroughly national revival of the Gothic style. In sentiment and in detail it neither offended by its violence nor sacrificed English to modern sympathies. If not remarkable for its originality, or its energy, it was always pleasing, moderate and sensible. Indeed it had, in common with its author, a geniality that was eminently impressed upon everything he did.[60]

Scott's churches were certainly not as adventurous in design as those by his former pupils, Street and Bodley – the latter describing his own early church in Brighton later as

> a boyish antagonistic effort. Not believing in what one saw at Scott's one went in for a violent reaction. One had seen bad mouldings, and so would not have any, and inane crockets – one felt 'away with them' – which was but the weakness of youth.[61]

Some of Scott's churches exhibited the fashion for Italian Gothic and for structural polychromy. In fact, as it has recently been noticed, Scott was a pioneer in the use of multicoloured materials, for he had used brick diaper patterns in the Tudor manner on several of his workhouses.[62] And he returned to brick polychromy in the 1850s. There is, for instance, his church at Dresden in Stoke-on-Trent of 1853 which Nikolaus Pevsner found 'an architectural mystery': red brick, 'very loudly diapered', with an interior of yellow brick with red stripes combined with a polygonal apse with radiating gables with timber bargeboards (is the answer that the design was devolved to an imaginative assistant?).[63] Perhaps his most Ruskinian creation was the apse built on to the Camden Chapel in Camberwell, a Georgian brick box, in 1854, a project in which Ruskin, who lived nearby, took a close interest (as he had earlier with the rebuilding of St Giles). This colourful addition was not Gothic, however, but in a round-arched, Italian Romanesque style.

Just as Ruskin would become disillusioned with Scott (and architects in general), so Scott himself would come to object to 'Ruskinism, such as would make Ruskin's very hair stand upon end; Butterfieldianism gone mad with its endless stripings of red and black bricks'. Quite early in his career Scott declared against the 'mere eccentricity' which would make, for modern eyes, some High Victorian Gothic more interesting, especially the work of those architects whom Goodhart-Rendel characterised as 'Rogues', desperately striving after originality. In a lecture given in 1848, Scott observed that there were architects who seemed

> in their designs to be ever studying where they can, with or without any reasonable excuse, introduce little oddities and freaks of fancy, such as we occasionally observe in old buildings. They seem to scorn an ordinary material, or a good straightforward door or window, as the vulgar, every-day refuge of uninventive minds, and to imagine that genius can alone exhibit itself in other features than those which have usually been resorted to . . . It is clear that this striving after quaintness and oddity is not one of the paths to healthful development.[64]

OPPOSITE FAR LEFT: The crossing of Chichester Cathedral soon after the collapse of the tower and spire in 1861.

OPPOSITE LEFT: Scott's rather Ruskinian design for the apse to be added to the Camden Chapel in Camberwell: woodcut from *The Builder*, 1854.

Scott's restoration work was also growing in parallel with the demand for new churches, for the revival of the Church of England also demanded that old and often much-abused churches be repaired and made fit for modern, dignified worship. Such commissions had begun in the days of Scott and Moffatt. The first such job was the refitting of Chesterfield Church in 1842. Soon after came the restoration of St Mary's Chapel on the Medieval bridge at Wakefield. Here he learned an unfortunate lesson. Having recovered the original design of the decayed chantry chapel front, Scott was persuaded, contrary to his own evolving principles, to recreate it entirely in new Caen stone and allow the old stonework to be set up as a front to 'the most precious of all boat-houses' in the grounds of Kettlethorpe Hall which, for Pevsner a century later, 'In its gentle decay . . . is the ideal of romantic garden furnishings.'[65] Soon the new front was as decayed as the old. 'I never repented but once, and that is ever since.'

The most important early restoration was that of St Mary's, Stafford, a cruciform church with an octagonal crossing tower. Scott was consulted in 1840, and work began two years later (see p. 44). Here, after much thought and investigation, he retained the Perpendicular low-pitched roof and clerestory over the nave but largely rebuilt the chancel and south transept, 'for embedded in the later walling we found abundant fragments of earlier work, which enabled me to reproduce the early English south transept with certainty, and a noble design it is'. For the antiquary, the Revd J. L. Petit, however, this was going too far and a 'useless waste of money'. A lengthy and informed correspondence ensued, and this 'discussion between two Conservatives, differing chiefly in the degree and definition of their conservatism' was printed in the splendid book, illustrated by a local artist and completed with a colour-lithographed frontispiece drawn by Pugin himself, which was published after the completion of the restoration (see p. 45).[66]

Scott regarded himself as a *conservative* restorer, as he explained in a lecture he gave at the first annual meeting of the Buckinghamshire Architectural and Archaeological Society in 1848, and published two years later as *A Plea for the Faithful Restoration of our Ancient Churches*. In it he observed that there were 'the "Conservative," the "Destructive" and the "Eclectic" systems of restoration' being practised and he regretted that his old adversary, the Ecclesiological Society, should have 'given an indirect sanction to this system of *radical restoration*', the 'Destructive'. This system appealed to the precedent of Medieval architects, who were happy to destroy the beautiful works of their predecessors in order to build something better and bigger. Scott had an answer to that.

> *Our position is . . .* totally distinct *from that of the ancient architects. They had been led by Providence to originate a new and wonderfully beautiful style of art, suited beyond any which had before existed to the uses of the church . . . Our own position is manifestly and totally different; we have not originated a new style, but are called upon to re-awaken one which has for centuries lain dormant; and it is absurd to argue that, because those who originated it did not scruple, during its progress, at destroying specimens of the earlier varieties, to make way for what they thought better, we are equally free to destroy their works to make way for our own.*

Scott stated his own position eloquently, regretting that some of his contemporaries were willing to destroy something they had only recently learned to appreciate.

> *In nothing is this want of humility seen so much as in church restoration. Nearly every restorer has his favourite style, or some fancy notion, to which he wishes to make everything subservient; and it is a most lamentable fact, that there has been far*

more done to obliterate genuine examples of pointed architecture, by the tampering caprices of well-meant restorations, than had been effected by centuries of mutilation and neglect. A restored church seems to lose all its truthfulness, and to become as little authentic, as an example of ancient art, as if it had been rebuilt on a new design. The restorer too often preserves only *just what he fancies, and alters even that if it does not quite suit his taste. He adds what features his caprice dictates and removes such as do not happen to please him, without the smallest consideration that the building should be treated with more veneration than if it had been erected yesterday. It is against this system of so-called restoration, a system which threatens to deprive us of all authentic examples of the humbler forms of this sacred art, that I wish to take this opportunity of PROTESTING.*

Scott was, however, well aware of the practical difficulties involved in carrying out a conservative repair, and, 'while I venture forward as a champion of conservatism, I cannot boast of having myself carried out its principles to my own satisfaction'. For a careful restoration was impossible without the cooperation of the incumbent, so often zealous to make his church comfortable and suitable for modern ideas for worship, while 'The practical workman *detests restoration*, and will always destroy and renew rather than preserve and restore.' And a neglected and decrepit building had to be made safe: 'One part of the church is found to be in worse condition than was expected, and, having to be rebuilt, the parties interested think that its design might be improved – one of the windows is an eyesore to the incumbent, or to some influential parishioner.'[67]

Scott's practice was responsible for the restoration of hundreds of old churches, and he has often been blamed for decisions which were beyond his control. The assumption is that he, like other restorers, was often guilty of replacing original features with ones in a better or earlier style, as prejudice or archaeological evidence demanded, but in a recent exhaustive study, Suzanne Branfoot could find only 'seven instances . . . out of the whole body of his 427 restorations [of churches] in England, where he removed what appear to have been genuine old stone windows and even those may have been replacements'.[68] Far from removing Perpendicular windows as a matter of course in favour of conjectural improvements, Scott often retained and repaired Perpendicular work. And it is clear that Scott cared and was closely involved in what he was doing. A letter survives from 1871 written to G. E. Street about the old stall seats in the chancel of Edgcott Church in Buckinghamshire, because the return only survived on the north side and the incumbent wanted to do away with this inconvenient anomaly. In this he was supported by the Oxford Diocesan Society. 'My dear Street,' Scott wrote, 'I have fought hard against this . . . can you help me in this? I value it no less for being humble. It is good old work & in its place, and I hold that it is wrong to remove it.'[69]

Scott was often guilty of removing Jacobean and later Classical furnishings, and he was responsible for transmogrifying Wren's St Michael's Cornhill by inserting Lombardic tracery in the windows and 'by the use of a sort of early Basilican style, to give a tone to the existing classic architecture'. Scott did, however, support a campaign to stop the demolition of many of the City of London churches, and seems to have been responsible for an anonymous pamphlet on the subject in 1854. His arguments were primarily pastoral, concerning the sacredness of their sites and their value as Christian symbols, but as a Gothic ecclesiologist, he could not regard these Classical buildings as

models of architecture, nor are they, for the most part, in the style best suited to ecclesiastical purposes. They are, however, singularly picturesque, both individually and in their grouping. They are generally the work of that great architect who seems to have been born for the very purpose of raising our city from its ashes.[70]

(Later, Edmund Ferrey recalled Scott warmly claiming that 'the forest of towers and spires was one of the glories of the city of London'.[71]) And it is much to his credit that Scott was also instrumental in 'saving St John's, Leeds – probably the most interesting church of the Jacobean period – from destruction'. (see p. 48) He also strongly supported the retention of Worcester's early eighteenth-century Guildhall when threatened with demolition in 1877.

Church restoration greatly concerned Scott for almost the whole of his career. He returned to the subject in 1862, when he delivered a lecture to RIBA, 'On the Conservation of Ancient Architectural Monuments and Remains'. In it he admitted that much was wrong with the widespread practice of restoration, while acknowledging, like many of his architect contemporaries, that the situation was so much worse in France.

I am . . . uncertain whether we do not all go upon a wrong principle in our dealings with ancient churches. I could almost wish the word 'restoration' expunged from our architectural vocabulary, and that we could be content with the more commonplace term 'reparation.' We have got into the way of assuming that the 'restoration' of a church must in its own nature be the signal for pulling it to pieces from top to bottom.[72]

In conclusion, Scott called for a 'vigilance committee' to work with antiquarian societies in trying to prevent abuses. This was heeded: in 1864 the RIBA Committee on the Conservation of Ancient Monuments and Remains was set up, with Scott on board, which would publish two documents of advice on the restoration or the repair and restoration of ancient buildings. (Earlier, Scott stated that he was 'in the habit of sending a copy of lithographed instructions' reflecting his general principles on restoration 'to clerks of works, &c., engaged in repairing old buildings'.[73])

By this time, Scott was involved with a majority of the ancient cathedrals in England and Wales. In 1847 he had 'received intelligence of my appointment as architect to the refitting, &c., of Ely Cathedral, which opened out before me a new field'. Two years later, 'wholly unexpectedly', he became Surveyor to Westminster Abbey, 'an appointment which has afforded me more pleasure than any other which I have held'. The results of his enthusiastic investigations into the venerable building were later published in a book, *Gleanings from Westminster Abbey* (edited by his friend J. H. Parker, with contributions from others including William Burges). Such was Scott's competence, and his ease and sympathy with most clergy, that other such appointments and consultancies soon followed. When, in 1861, the fragile crossing tower and spire of Chichester Cathedral collapsed owing to ill-advised interventions by a railway engineer, Scott was inevitably the expert to bring in to repair the damage, and he carefully reconstructed the steeple (heightening it slightly) using as many original stones as possible (see p. 50). In 1877, in the original manuscript of his *Recollections*, Scott made a 'list of cathedrals and other large churches of similar class which I have been by God's permission engaged upon'. These were: Ely Cathedral, Westminster Abbey, Hereford Cathedral, Lichfield Cathedral, Peterborough Cathedral, Salisbury Cathedral, Chichester Cathedral, Chester Cathedral, St David's Cathedral, St Asaph Cathedral, Bangor Cathedral, Gloucester Cathedral, Worcester Cathedral, Canterbury Cathedral ('in prospect'), St Albans Abbey, Tewkesbury Abbey, Ripon Cathedral, Beverley Minster, Bridlington Priory and Selby Abbey. And he had forgotten to include Exeter and Rochester, Christ Church Cathedral at Oxford and Bath Abbey.

Scott's contribution ranged from refurnishing or small repairs to large-scale reconstruction. Often he was acting as consultant and working with a local architect, continuing projects already begun. Even so, the amount of work involved was prodigious, as it necessitated initial investigations (sometimes requiring opening up parts of the fabric) and writing a report with recommendations; meeting the Dean and Chapter and perhaps addressing a public meeting to solicit support; frequent site visits, and having to deal with often difficult clergy and patrons as well as with the clerk of works. At Exeter, Scott privately confessed that, 'The Dean was so outrageous in his interference that I was driven nearly out of my senses – over and over again all through this work and really could not get any part of my own way without most wretched squabbling – which often made me perfectly ill and made me hate the very name of Exeter', and so he was reluctant to visit. At Salisbury, the new reredos was given by Lord Beauchamp, 'as unpleasant a man to do business with as ever I met with – a tyrant of the first water!', while the screen was partly paid for by Mrs Lear, who 'assumed from her very partial gift a power of tyrannizing only second to that assumed by Lord B.'.

These complicated and expensive building campaigns could go on for decades. At Ely, for instance, Scott began by moving and refurnishing the choir; the challenging restoration of the great Octagon – whose original appearance before eighteenth-century changes Scott recovered with considerable accuracy – was not commenced until 1859 and only completed after his death. In many cases, the changes wrought by Scott proved controversial as he displayed an intuitive genius in reconstructing original features on the basis both of archaeological evidence and his own profound knowledge of Medieval architecture, which sometimes may have been taken too far. All too often, however, it was the clergy who insisted on change. At Oxford, a modern and unsatisfactory east window was replaced by a conjectural Norman wheel window at the insistence of Dean Liddell (father of Alice, the inspiration for *Alice in Wonderland*) when Scott in his report stated that 'the design of the earlier windows was unique, but is so completely lost excepting only the mere fact of a great circle having existed, to be quite beyond recovery' and recommended restoring the later fourteenth-century window tracery, for which there was more evidence.[74] As for St Albans, almost everything modern, ugly and wrong was the work of the arrogant, rich patron, Lord Grimthorpe, most of it achieved after the much-abused Scott was no longer around to object.

Scott also displayed genius in his understanding of structure, often having to stabilise and strengthen large structures that were in a deplorable state of repair. Occasionally he worked with engineers, notably Frederick Sheilds, who helped him strap together with diagonal iron ties the crossing tower at Salisbury and replace the shattered stonework stone by stone. The result, Scott wrote, 'is a very fine engineering work. We dare not, however, touch the piers below which buckle inwards at mid-height. They must be *watched* and strutted if needful. I trust *not!*' Some of the works Scott undertook, underpinning walls and unstable towers, or straightening leaning walls, were impressive in scale – and alarming. In defending himself against the Anti-Restoration '*do-nothing*' approach, Scott noted that he had 'had the happiness of saving several noble towers imminently threatened with destruction . . . I do not covet such work: – one sleeps more quietly without it'. Two of those towers were at Ripon, where

The western towers had sunk dreadfully, and were split from top to bottom on three sides (if not four). The cracks were nearly a foot wide. We underbuilt the walls for some twelve feet below their old foundations, propping them up meanwhile with an enormous mass of timber shoring. The danger was terrific. At one time a perfect

*avalanche of rubble roared in upon the men engaged below from the centre of the wall
over their heads. Thank God, however, it was effected in safety.*

Restorations were not just concerned with structure. Ancient and often much-
altered cathedrals had to be made suitable for modern Anglican choral worship, and this
sometimes involved moving and refurnishing the choir as well as installing (or restoring)
a suitable reredos. It was often desired to have a division made between nave and chancel,
but without making the latter inaccessible to the laity as ancient stone screens (sometimes
removed by the Georgians) did. The answer was an open screen. On several occasions
Scott declared that, 'My principle is not to destroy an *old* close rood screen, nor to erect
a *new* one.' At Ely, his first cathedral, he installed one of timber, 'the first case in which
an open screen had been adopted in our cathedrals, and I devoted infinite pains to its
design'. But Scott soon concluded that metal was the only material which would meet

conflicting practical and aesthetic demands. He designed open metal screens for Salisbury and Lichfield, but the most remarkable was that designed for Hereford Cathedral and made by Scott's favourite metalworker, Francis Skidmore of Coventry. This extraordinary object was, in fact, made of iron, copper, brass, mosaic, enamels, cut and polished stones and marble. Skidmore offered to make it at a reduced price if it could be exhibited at the 1862 International Exhibition in South Kensington, which it was, the *Illustrated London News* considering it to be 'the most noble work of modern times . . . a monument of surpassing skill of our land and our age'.[75]

Scott himself later had doubts about it, writing that 'Skidmore followed my design, but somewhat aberrantly. It is a fine work, but too loud and self-asserting for an English church'. Scott was much concerned with the revival of the various crafts – 'the subsidiary arts' – that were integral to the success of a modern Gothic and wrote about them, in his *Recollections* and elsewhere. He took a close interest in the development of stained glass, and wrote about the artists he knew and worked with, notably Clayton and Bell (Alfred Bell being a former pupil), but also John Hardman ('or rather his artist [John Hardman] Powell') who 'had the advantage or disadvantage of a long drilling under Pugin. It made him a first-rate glass-painter.' With regard to decorative colouring, Scott thought that there had not been much advance since Pugin, and that, 'Our architects must become artists and then, and not till then, shall we have a chance of success.' As for encaustic tiling, 'we have made little progress since Pugin's time'.

Scott was particularly interested in improving the art of architectural sculpture, and regarded figure sculpture as an integral part of his architecture. Benedict Read has written that, 'The quality of the artists Scott employed for figure sculpture when it was feasible would seem to confirm his serious regard for it.'[76] In particular there was John Birnie Philip, who collaborated with Scott on new sculpture required by a number of cathedral restorations, and who was responsible for some of the tympani on the Whitehall front of the Government Offices, for part of the frieze on the Albert Memorial and much else. Other good sculptors used by Scott included H. H. Armstead and James Redfern, who both worked on the Albert Memorial. (In 1877 Scott lamented the untimely end of Redfern, noting that, 'He was one of four sculptors whom I had known to have died in poverty within about two years!'. The others were Philip, Theodore Phyffers and Alfred Stevens.) Much of the work done for him by Philip, in particular, was ornamental rather than figurative, and Scott believed that 'I have done as much as most men to forward the art of carving . . . I have had a vast deal of bad carving done for me, it is true, some of it detestable. This has been mainly owing to the extent of my business, which has been always too much for my capacity of attending to it.' Harry Hems was one of several good craftsmen used by Scott, who praised in particular what had been achieved by William Brindley, of the firm of Farmer and Brindley, and considered that his work on some of Scott's own buildings were 'examples of carving of a very high order'. In this context, it is intriguing that, in a sketchbook, Scott praised the new Sacristy nest to Notre-Dame in Paris by Viollet-le-Duc as 'perhaps the most perfectly finished Gothic building of Modern Times... It is late 13th-century work and carved out as finely as is possible... The carving is probably the best of modern times and should be seen by English carvers.'

Unlike G. E. Street, who provided drawings for every detail and sought absolute overall control, Scott was prepared to give some creative responsibility to craftsmen and did his work 'by influence' – an attitude which might seem to anticipate the approach of the later Arts and Crafts movement. What he felt was important was for carvers to study natural foliage and the best models from the past. To this end, in addition to his many other activities, he became much involved with the creation of the Architectural

Museum in 1852, leading a campaign also supported by Ruskin to acquire the collection of Medieval specimens assembled by the architect Lewis Nockalls Cottingham as a nucleus. It has been suggested that this idea was inspired by attitudes to craftsmanship he had encountered in Germany, and the use of a *Bauhütte* (construction shed) for the completion of Cologne Cathedral, which contained casts from old carving and from nature, although a similar set-up had been established by Pugin for building the New Palace of Westminster.[77]

With the support of the Prince Consort, the resulting collection was established in a wharf at Cannon Row in Westminster and there, for a few years, 'were our carvers taught their art from the best ancient models, and our students acquired a degree of skill and taste in the drawing of architectural ornament which had never before been reached, nor has (since the removal of the museum) been retained'. Evidence of this are the capitals in Scott's church at Trefnant in Wales, carved by J. Blinstone of Denbigh, (see p. 123) who

(see p. 123)

> *studied for some days, under Mr Scott's direction, the specimens of French carving of the thirteenth century, collected in the Architectural Museum in London, and on his return successfully applied the same principles to his own work, arranging every group of leaves from natural specimens gathered as they were needed from the woods and hedges around.*[78]

Scott made great efforts on behalf of the museum and he was bitter about its eventual failure, owing to the lack of financial support, and its partial absorption by the South Kensington Museum, although it was later revived as a separate institution, the Royal Architectural Museum, in Westminster in 1869 with Scott as Treasurer; he also wrote a guide to the collection.

Scott's contribution to the Gothic Revival was also literary, notably his book, *Remarks on Secular & Domestic Architecture, Present & Future*, which was published in 1857 (and was so successful that a second edition came out the following year). Scott, like Pugin before him, argued that Gothic, although the Christian style, was not just for churches but should be used for all types of building. He wrote the book, he explained, because 'the vernacular Domestic architecture of our day is wholly unworthy of our state of civilization, and requires a thorough reformation', and because 'the success, however incomplete, of the great movement by which Pointed architecture has been revived for ecclesiastical purposes . . . has not hitherto had full scope for producing a corresponding effect upon our secular buildings'. One problem, however, was that England, though so rich in Medieval churches, had few available precedents for a secular Gothic architecture. So, on the title page, famous Continental examples were illustrated: the Cloth Hall at Ypres for the North of Europe, and the Doge's Palace and the Palazzo Pubblico in Siena for the South, while the text concluded with a note 'On the uses to be made of the Mediaeval Architecture of Italy'.

Scott was at pains to deny that the Gothic Revival was an antiquarian movement, seeking to revive all that was ancient, when in fact it was

> *pre-eminently free, comprehensive, and practical; ready to adapt itself to every change in the habits of society, to embrace every new material or system of construction, and to adopt implicitly and naturally, and with hearty good will, every invention or improvements, whether artistic, constructional, or directed to the increase of comfort and convenience.*

Nor need the secular Gothic architect necessarily feel obliged exclusively to use the pointed arch. Windows could be capped by a straight lintel, and 'our future architecture' should 'embrace, and that heartily, the two leading forms – the round and the pointed arch'. And much as Scott was fond of 'pattern-glazing' and the 'old system of quarries and lead lights', he was happy to fill those windows with 'plate-glass, as undivided as possible. It is one of the most useful and beautiful inventions of our day, and eminently calculated to give cheerfulness to our houses.'

As for new materials, far from being hostile to the use of iron as a structural element, as Ruskin and Pugin would seem to have been, Scott was always keen on it. The architectural problem now was to integrate metal forms into the Gothic language, and Scott maintained that, 'It is self-evident that this triumph of modern metallic construction opens out a perfectly new field for architectural development.' He had been familiar with iron structures since his early experience working on the Hungerford Market, a Classical building. But he denied that 'modern engineering' belonged to one style of architecture more than any other.

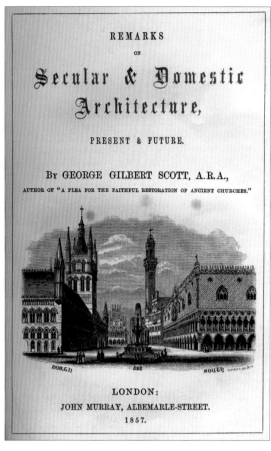

> *People fancy that, because they have grown up during the prevalence of our modern classicism, they have something to do with it. I deny this in toto. Is not an iron bridge, or an iron roof, more allied to medieval timber construction, than to any works we know of classic antiquity? Has a suspension-bridge any nearer relation to the Parthenon than to Westminster Hall? . . . Then, again, of the iron and glass structures so much in vogue, – are they especially Grecian, Roman or Renaissance in their idea? What should we say, for instance, of their great type, the Crystal Palace? Is it more like a Grecian temple, or a Gothic cathedral? The fact is, that all these iron constructions are, if anything, more suited to Gothic than classic architecture.*

ABOVE: The title page of Scott's influential book on secular Gothic published in 1857.

Scott would go on triumphantly to demonstrate how iron structures could be integrated with modern Gothic at St Pancras Station.[79]

'I am no mediaevalist,' Scott insisted. 'I do not advocate the styles of the middle ages as such. If we had a distinctive architecture of our own day worthy of the greatness of our age, I should be content to follow it; but we have not.' And Scott, thoughtful and intelligent as he was, suggested one reason why not.

> *The peculiar characteristic of the present day, as compared with all former periods, is this, – that we are acquainted with the history of art. We know better whence each nation of antiquity derived its arts than they ever knew themselves, and can trace out with precision the progressions of which those who were their prime movers were almost unconscious . . . It is reserved to us, alone of all the generations of the human race, to know perfectly our own standing-point, and to look back upon a perfect history of what has gone before us, tracing out all the changes in the arts of the past as clearly as if every scene in its long drama were re-enacted before our eyes. This is amazingly interesting to us as a matter of amusement and erudition, but I fear it is a hindrance rather than a help to us as artists.[80]*

ABOVE: Scott's competition
entry in the Government
Offices competition of 1857:
a woodcut from *The Builder*
of the perspective of the
internal quadrangle.

This truth should be borne in mind when contemplating both the unhappy attempts by some of Scott's contemporaries to create a 'Victorian' style, and the condescension of our own day towards architectural revivalism of earlier periods.

Apart from the early workhouses, Scott's first secular buildings were vicarages and schools; these were much influenced by the work of Pugin. Now, with the publication of his book on domestic architecture, commissions for large country houses began to come his way. The best known was Kelham Hall near Newark in Nottinghamshire, rebuilt after a fire in 1857. Here Scott put his ideas into practice: there is plate glass and exposed iron beams, together with a bewildering variety of window forms. Determined asymmetry suggests a practical, Puginian approach, but Kelham, built of a hard red brick, can never have been successful as a country house and, indeed, it later served as offices for the local authority. As Mark Girouard wrote in his study *The Victorian Country House*, 'as a private house it was an absurdity because Scott was unable, architecturally speaking, to stop preaching a sermon or addressing a public meeting . . . It is scarcely secular, and not at all domestic.'[81] Although Scott would go on to design several more large Gothic houses which have some impressive interiors and grand staircases, the fact is that he had no experience of planning a country house – a complex matter in the Victorian period – and the results were not endearing. It is not surprising that the next generation, including Scott's own architect sons, would reject such ponderous Gothic in favour of more domestic-looking styles. The most successful of these houses was Walton Hall in Warwickshire (today a hotel), built of a fine local stone, but perhaps it is more interesting for having been the scene of one of the great Victorian sex scandals: that involving Scott's client, Sir Charles Mordaunt, his young wife and the Prince of Wales.[82]

Scott was much more successful in designing public buildings, and an opportunity for this came while he was writing his book with the announcement of a competition for the design of new Government Offices in Whitehall. What followed was one of the worst-run architectural competitions ever held, and an object lesson in how not to commission and build a major public work. It is a complicated, farcical story and it cost Scott much in

effort, time and reputation although he did eventually manage to build the new Foreign Office, though not in Gothic. The heated parliamentary and public debate about the style of the offices successive governments proposed to erect between Whitehall and St James's Park was the principal engagement in the so-called 'Battle of the Styles' between Gothic and Classic. As Scott's opponent and nemesis, the Prime Minister, Lord Palmerston, put it in 1861, 'the battle of the books, the battle of the Big and Little Endians, and the battle of the Green Ribbands and the Blue Ribbands at Constantinople were all as nothing compared with this battle of the Gothic and Palladian styles'.[83]

A new building for the Foreign Office had long been mooted and the project gained momentum after Palmerston became Prime Minister for the first time in 1855, in the middle of the Crimean War. A competition was announced the following year, but, absurdly, in three parts: for a general plan for the Whitehall area, for a new Foreign Office and for a new War Office, the conduct of the campaign against Russia having exposed the inadequacies of the civil service. Scott submitted designs for both offices in a combined scheme. He later wrote how he set himself

> to design the elements which I thought best suited to a public building. I designed windows suited to all positions, and of all varieties of size, form, and grouping; doorways, cornices, parapets, and imaginary combinations of all these, carefully studying to make them all thoroughly practical, and suited to this class of building. I did not aim at making my style 'Italian Gothic'; my ideas ran much more upon the French, to which for some years I had devoted my chief study. I did, however, aim at gathering a few hints from Italy, such as the pillar-mullion, the use of differently-coloured materials, and of inlaying. I also aimed at another thing which people consider Italian – I mean a certain squareness and horizontality of outline. This I consider pre-eminently suited to the street front of a public building. I combined this, however, with gables, high-pitched roofs, and dormers.

ABOVE: Scott's entry in the Government Offices competition: his perspective of his design for the Whitehall (War Office) front, 1857.

DESIGN FOR THE PROPOSED NEW FOREIGN OFFICE: FRONT NEXT ST. JAMES'S PARK.——Mr. G. G. Scott, A.R.A. Architect.

ABOVE: The St James's
Park front of Scott's
Gothic design for the
Foreign Office: woodcut
from *The Builder*, 1859.

OPPOSITE ABOVE:

A watercolour perspective,
possibly by J. D. Wyatt, of
Scott's adopted Gothic design
for the Foreign Office, revised
with Matthew Digby Wyatt,
showing the quadrangle.

OPPOSITE BELOW:

The entrance to the Foreign
Office within the quadrangle
in Scott's revised Gothic
design: woodcut from
The Builder 1859.

All in vain. Scott thought that the judges, 'who knew amazingly little about their subject were not Gothicly disposed', and they placed his design for the Foreign Office third. First came 'a flash affair by my old pupil Coe' (of Coe and Hofland); Banks and Barry (Charles Barry junior) came second with a Classical design, 'far from any good as I think'. As for the War Office, Henry Garling came first with another Classical scheme. However, it was clear almost from the start that the whole scheme was impractical and expensive and would never go ahead – especially after news of a serious revolt in India began to come through in 1857. Palmerston set the whole thing aside and appointed James Pennethorne, that excellent official architect who had earlier prepared a grand scheme for Whitehall, to design the new Foreign Office. At this, Scott 'thought myself at liberty to stir' and, with others, so stirred up the Institute of British Architects, of which he was then senior Vice-President, that petitions were sent and a deputation went to Parliament to protest about this offhand treatment of the architectural profession.

Meanwhile, early in 1858, Palmerston's government had resigned and was succeeded by a Conservative administration under Lord Derby, which appointed a Select Committee to look into the whole convoluted affair. It was chaired by A. J. Beresford Hope MP, who, as a founder of the Cambridge Camden Society, sometime editor of *The Ecclesiologist* and the patron for the building of Butterfield's All Saints, Margaret Street, was rather more sympathetic towards the Gothic cause. This committee found that, at one stage, Scott had been considered in second place for both the Foreign and War Offices. The eventual result was that, in November 1858, Lord John Manners, the new First Commissioner of Works, announced that Scott would be the architect for the proposed new Foreign Office.

Meanwhile, the War Office had dropped out of the picture but the new India Office, created by Disraeli's Government of India Act following the 'Indian Mutiny', had come in, along with its architect, Matthew Digby Wyatt, surveyor to the old East India Company. Scott and Wyatt agreed to work together to achieve a single coherent building on the proposed site south of Downing Street.

Scott's appointment did not go unchallenged, however, and a debate started about the merits and drawbacks of building in Gothic which, for many, had uncomfortable associations with the High Church party and Roman Catholicism. In a debate in the House of Commons, Palmerston, as leader of the opposition, wondered whether, if the grounds for Scott being given the job were applied to horse racing, 'the horse which ran second in two heats were held to be entitled to the cup'? He also protested that to choose Gothic was 'going back to the barbarism of the dark ages for a building which ought to belong to the times in which we live'.[84] Scott, ever anxious to justify himself and to respond to criticism, then made the mistake of hurriedly writing a bumptious letter to *The Times* to counter the accusation that his design was gloomy and insufficiently lit. In fact, he claimed, his proposed windows were larger than most prominent Classical buildings in London, and, 'as to cheerfulness of character, I really think that any unprejudiced person would come to the conclusion that, if compared with the Post Office, the Museum, the Palace, or even the Board of Trade or Whitehall Chapel, my design

ABOVE: Scott's perspective of
the St James's Park front of
his 'Byzantine' design for the
Foreign Office.

OPPOSITE ABOVE: Scott's
perspective of the Whitehall
front of his 'Byzantine' design
for the Foreign Office.

OPPOSITE BELOW:
A perspective of the
St James's Park front of
Scott's final, Classical design
for the Foreign and India
Offices which was accepted
by Lord Palmerston and
Parliament in 1861.

would carry the palm in this respect'.[85] This arrogant assertion, essentially that he was a better architect than not only the designers of recent major public buildings – Smirke, Blore and Barry – but also Inigo Jones, did not go down well. It infuriated Palmerston's 'private tutor in matters of architectural lore', Professor T. L. Donaldson, a founder of the Institute of Architects, who then proposed asking the Institute to reconsider the recommendation to award its Royal Gold Medal to Scott.

But worse was to follow. In June 1859, after a General Election and losing a vote of no confidence, the Conservative government resigned and Palmerston returned as Prime Minister: as Scott melodramatically put it, 'my arch-opponent became once more autocrat of England'. By this time Scott and Wyatt had prepared a design developed from Scott's competition scheme with the two offices facing each other across a large quadrangle, and tenders were out. But Palmerston soon summoned Scott,

and told me in a jaunty way that he could have nothing to do with this Gothic style, and that though he did not want to disturb my appointment, he must insist on my making a design in the Italian style, which he felt sure I could do quite as well as the other. That he heard I was so tremendously successful in the Gothic style, that if he let me alone I should Gothicize the whole country, &c., &c., &c.

Scott attempted to change Palmerston's mind, but the Prime Minister was of an older generation, a septuagenarian who wanted something 'more like modern architecture' and that, for him, meant something Classical. He wrote to Scott that

I could not contemplate without alarm the idea of filling up with gloomy looking

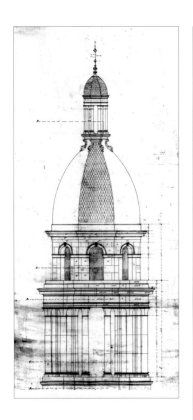

ABOVE: Scott's unexecuted design for the domed corner towers, which should have completed the Whitehall front of the Home & Colonial Offices.

buildings in the Gothic style, [the] whole of the space between Downing Street and Great George Street. With regard to the change to be made in the style of the elevations, I cannot entertain the smallest doubt that an architect of your known talent and ability will find it an easy task to design an elevation in the Italian or Classic style.[86]

The debate continued, both in Parliament and in the press. Scott had influential supporters. One rather ambivalent ally was John Ruskin, who wrote privately that

I think him an able and admirable architect – as far as architects reach in these days – I like his book exceedingly – much better than some of my own . . . But I do not care to stir in the question, because neither Scott nor anyone else can build either Gothic or Italian at present – all real work in those styles depends principally on the making of figure sculpture – all modern architecture is spurious, and must remain so until architects become sculptors.[87]

There was much infighting and intrigue, to which Scott devoted many aggrieved pages in his *Recollections*. But Scott himself was guilty of publishing an anonymous pamphlet, entitled *The Gothic Renaissance: Its Origin, Progress, and Principles*, which not only vaunted the merits of the style but also his own merits as an architect; as much of the text was taken from his book, *Secular & Domestic Architecture*, and from his recent Royal Academy lectures, his authorship must surely have been blatant.[88] As he later admitted, 'I did everything that a man could do, nearly my entire time being devoted to the fight.'

Scott's principal opponents were Donaldson and the wealthy architect, MP William Tite, along with Charles Barry junior, who had every reason to agitate as he had come second in the original competition for the Foreign Office, that is, ahead of Scott. Many MPs and fellow architects supported Scott, but a delegation of architects opposed to the Gothic also went to see Palmerston. Scott later wrote that he had not ceased to feel 'that the conduct of those architects who attended on this deputation was in a high degree unprofessional'. Others agreed: *Building News* announced that it was 'the greatest scandal and disgrace that has ever been inflicted on the architectural profession', and that Scott was 'the victim of a combination of envious rivals as selfish as it is ignoble'. But it was no good: in August 1859

Lord Palmerston sent for me, and, seating himself down before me in the most easy, fatherly way, said, 'I want to talk to you quietly, Mr Scott, about this business. I have been thinking a great deal about it, and I really think there was much force in what your friends said.' I was delighted at his supposed conversion. 'I really do think that there is a degree of inconsistency in compelling a Gothic architect to erect a classic building, and so I have been thinking of appointing you a coadjutor, who would in fact make the design!' I was thrown to the earth again.

(It later emerged that this 'coadjutor' would have been Garling, who, after all, had won the competition for the War Office).

Scott then retired to Scarborough with his wife and family.

I was thoroughly out of health, through the badgering, anxiety, and bitter disappointment which I had gone through, and for the first time since commencing practice, twenty-four years before, I gave myself a quasi-holiday of two months, with sea air and a course of quinine.

What to do?

I saw that, with Lord Palmerston, Gothic would have no chance, and I had agreed to prepare an Italian design . . . To resign would be to give up a sort of property which Providence had placed in the hands of my family, and would be simply rewarding my professional opponents for their unprecedented attempt to wrest a work from the hands of a brother architect.

The solution was compromise: 'to prepare a design in a variety of Italian, as little inconsistent with my antecedents as possible'. It had to be round-arched, so Scott began to study the 'Byzantine of the early Venetian palaces' and the earliest Renaissance buildings of Venice, and came up with a Byzantine manner 'toned into a more modern and usable form, by reference to those examples of the renaissance which had been influenced by the presence of Byzantine works'. Scott prepared a design in this style, which he would use elsewhere, notably for the chapel at King's College, London. He then revised the design after consulting C. R. Cockerell, William Burn and James Ferguson. But it wouldn't do. In September 1860, Scott was summoned again by Palmerston, who

told me that he did not wish to disturb my position, but he would have nothing to do with Gothic; and as to the style of my recent design, it was 'neither one thing nor t'other – a regular mongrel affair – and he would have nothing to do with it either:' that he must insist on my making a design in the ordinary Italian, and that, though he had no wish to displace me, he nevertheless, if I refused, must cancel my appointment.

There was nothing else for it. Scott

bought some costly books on Italian architecture, and set vigorously to work to rub up what, though I had once understood pretty intimately, I had allowed to grow rusty by twenty years' neglect . . . I went to Paris and studied the Louvre and most of the important buildings, and really recovered some of my lost feelings for the style . . . I was so determined to show myself not behindhand with the classicists that I seemed to have more power than usual.

Both the Foreign Office and the India Office were now to face St James's Park, and a picturesque composition was now possible owing to the decision by the government to demolish the State Paper Office, a most interesting late work by Soane, which left an irregular building line. This composition, with a curved linking quadrant and a belvedere tower, was 'suggested by a sketch of Mr Digby Wyatt's'. Wyatt, who was entirely responsible for the interior of the India Office, had 'disinterestedly' urged Scott to make a Classical design, as Scott acknowledged, 'for had I resigned he would beyond a doubt have had the whole design of the India Office, instead of half of it, committed to his hands'.

The resulting building is impressive, with the Classical language given a slightly Gothic tone in many of the details. In fact, Scott's approach to architectural composition was often rather Classical in character in terms of symmetry and regularity; he had, after all, enjoyed a good Classical training with Edmeston and Roberts. The rather contrived external asymmetries and irregular fenestration rhythms, ostensibly expressing internal arrangements, which appeared on the first Gothic design for the Government Offices (and which were bound to offend Palmerston) were not really typical of his secular work. Inside the Foreign Office, Scott was able both to create grand Classical spaces

ABOVE: The Foreign and India Offices as
Scott would have preferred them to be:
a perspective Scott had made of his final
design translated into Gothic which he
submitted to the Royal Academy of Arts
as his Diploma Work and was exhibited
in 1864.

and to use exposed iron beams – as his theories demanded. The Ambassadors' Staircase and the generous and richly decorated public rooms, in particular the double-height, barrel-vaulted Grand Reception Room, are splendid; Beresford Hope later described the building as 'a kind of national palace, or drawing room for the nation, with working rooms hung on to it for foreign business of the country'.[89]

Scott's Classical design was approved by the House of Commons in July 1861 'after a very stout fight by the Gothic party, who naturally and consistently opposed it strenuously'. To salve his conscience, Scott had a coloured perspective drawing made to demonstrate how the plan and outline of the building was 'even more suited to the Gothic style than the old one . . . It was by very far superior to any which I had hitherto made, and I placed it with my other Gothic designs in the exhibition at the Royal Academy, as a silent protest against what was going on.' (See pp. 68-69) The eastern half of the site was now allotted to the Home and Colonial Offices. Scott was officially appointed architect for these in 1868, but his design was never entirely completed: economies imposed by Gladstone's notorious First Commissioner, A. S. Ayrton, in 1870 resulted in the omission of the intended porte cochère and the corner towers and cupolas on the Whitehall front. As Scott later complained, these were 'much needed to relieve the monotony of so vast a group. I live in hopes of their restitution' – but he lived in vain. Perhaps it is indicative of attitudes to architecture in England that nobody today seems to notice their absence (see p. 66).

T. G. Jackson, who made a perspective of the final Foreign Office design for Scott, later wrote that 'though he nearly broke his heart about it, I think that building is the finest thing he ever did'.[90] The whole lengthy and exhausting affair brought out both the best and the worst in Scott. He knew that he had lost some moral authority by caving in and abandoning the Gothic cause to keep the job.

I felt that I should be irreparably injured if I were to lose a work thus publicly placed in my hands, and I was step by step driven into the most annoying position of carrying out my largest work in a style contrary to the direction of my life's labours. My shame and sorrow were for a time extreme, but, to my surprise, the public seemed to understand my position and to feel for it, and I never received any annoying or painful rebuke, and even Mr Ruskin told me I had done quite right.

What is certain is that Scott's business was not affected as jobs continued to roll in. He may no longer have been considered in the avant-garde of what he called the 'Gothic Renaissance', but he was now well known and respected, definitely part of the establishment. In 1862 he was one of seven architects – and the only Gothic Revivalist – asked to submit designs for a memorial to the late Prince Consort. The following year Queen Victoria approved the advice of the Memorial Committee and selected 'a magnificent design by Mr Scott, for a Gothic cross'. There were some dissenting voices, notably that of the Prime Minister, Lord Palmerston, who did not like any of the designs and would have preferred 'an open Grecian temple' containing a statue of Albert, but the prejudices of Scott's 'arch-opponent' did not carry much weight with the Queen. Scott's selection was a triumph both personally and for the Gothic cause. A splendid model and drawings of the proposed memorial were on show in the Exposition Universelle held in Paris in 1867, and *Building News* noted that Scott had 'a stall all to himself, but he is a favoured individual, and a sort of royal personage, being an immortaliser of Prince Albert, and South Kensington dare not quite extinguish him'.[91]

Scott's general conception, of a Gothic canopy with a spire sheltering the statue of the Prince, was not at all original. G. M. Kemp's monument to Sir Walter Scott in Edinburgh was an obvious precedent, and Scott may well have been influenced by seeing the published design by Thomas Worthington for the Albert Memorial in Manchester. What was novel, however, was Scott's interpretation of the idea, integrating architecture with sculpture, combining many crafts by using metal, mosaic and enamel as well as stone, marble and granite. He proposed

> *the realization in an actual edifice, of the architectural designs furnished by the metal-work shrines of the middle ages. Those exquisite productions of the goldsmith and the jeweller profess in nearly every instance to be models of architectural structures, yet no such structures exist, nor, so far as we know, ever did exist . . . They are architecture as elaborated by the mind and the hand of the jeweller; an exquisite phantasy realized only to the small scale of the model. My notion, whether good or bad, was for once to realize this jeweller's architecture in a structure of full size, and this has furnished the key-note of my design and of its execution.*

When the memorial was unveiled – without John Foley's gilded seated figure of the Prince – a decade later, it provoked both praise and scorn from critics. Praise came from *The Times*: 'Were the Albert Memorial but the work of some former age, did it but stand in Florence, or Munich, or Paris, or in any other capital but our own, every English critic would call it beautiful.' But several influential critics thought otherwise, and by 1872 the architectural climate was changing and the crest of the wave that had carried Scott and his design to success was breaking. Emmett, in his (anonymous) *Quarterly Review* attack, dismissed 'the Hyde Park trophy', and in the *Pall Mall Gazette* (again anonymously) Sidney Colvin, soon to be Slade Professor of Fine Art and director of the Fitzwilliam Museum at Cambridge, described the memorial as 'organic nullity disguised beneath superficial exuberance'.[92] 'I can only say that if this work is worthy of their contempt,' responded Scott, 'I am myself equally deserving of it, for it is the result of my highest and most enthusiastic efforts.' He should not have worried: the Albert Memorial was a popular success, and it secured him a knighthood.

Scott was also given many opportunities to try out the secular Gothic manner he had developed, in vain, for the Foreign Office. The principal example is the Midland Grand Hotel at St Pancras Station, built largely of red brick, which 'was in the same style which I had almost originated several years earlier, for the government offices, but divested of the Italian element'. Scott may have been disappointed that this opportunity was for a commercial rather than a public or civic function, but 'I was glad to be able to erect one building in that style in London'. He had been invited in 1865 to enter a limited competition for the hotel by a friend who was a director of the Midland Railway, and Scott was given the job even though the estimated cost of his design exceeded the one specified (and, in the event, a whole floor had to be omitted). It was clear that this ambitious railway company wanted its prominent London hotel to be designed by a famous architect, just as it was prepared to pay for a train shed which, at 243 feet, was for a time the largest unsupported span in the world. And Scott was pleased to find that, 'as if by anticipation its section was a pointed arch'.

The secular Gothic style was employed elsewhere, sometimes for buildings all of stone and sometimes for buildings of red brick with a touch of polychromatic decoration. It was used for the new town hall at Preston, Lancashire, which had a clock tower similar to that at St Pancras; for the Leeds Infirmary, built to the pavilion plan recommended by

Florence Nightingale, and Beckett's Bank in the same city; for the Fitzroy Library at Lewes in Sussex and for the library at Harrow School. Scott worked extensively in both ancient English universities: at Exeter and New Colleges in Oxford, and at King's and St John's Colleges in Cambridge, designing libraries and residential buildings and sometimes restoring the old halls and chapels. In 1864 he received the valuable commission to design ambitious new buildings for the University of Glasgow on a new site. Here his Gothic manner included certain Scottish Baronial features – tourelles and crow-stepped gables – to create 'a style which I may call my own invention, having already initiated it in the Albert Institute in Dundee'. At the same time he was also asked to design buildings for the new university in Bombay. With all this work, he really need not have been so disappointed that he did not win the limited competition for the new Royal Courts of Justice in London held in 1866 – 'a great failure' (see p. 77). Other architects surely deserved a chance, and the job eventually went to his old pupil, G. E. Street.

The library and convocation hall of the University of Bombay are among the most impressive buildings in a city, which, in the 1860s, was given a number of Gothic Revival public buildings, mostly designed by British architects and engineers resident in India. Bombay was not, however, mentioned in Scott's *Recollections*. This was because he resigned the commission in a huff, and the buildings were completed by others. The designs were sent out in 1866, and Scott explained that the style was 'a free variety of the architecture of the thirteenth century' adapted to the 'exigencies of a hot climate. He proposed open cloisters and verandas and a 'double roof' over the hall. Unfortunately, it was difficult for an architect in London to estimate the cost of building in Bombay, and the syndicate was shocked to learn that Scott's design would cost three times as much as the funds available, so it 'decided to avail itself of the experience of local architects for reducing the cost'. Scott was furious, writing back that: 'It is customary, after an architect had at a great amount of labour and study, prepared a design, to request him to make any reductions which may be thought necessary to meet any difficulties as to the outlay', and had nothing more to do with the job after he had received his fee and expenses. As built, the convocation hall is as much the work of George Twigge-Molecey and Walter Paris as of Scott, but the library, with its open Gothic loggias and open spiral staircases and magnificent tall tower, is probably largely as Scott designed.[93]

The Bombay commission was one of several in British colonies that suggest Scott might be regarded as an Imperial architect, although he never travelled beyond Western Europe. He designed splendid tomb monuments for Lady Canning, wife of the Viceroy, in Calcutta and for Sir Charles Hotham, Governor of Victoria, in Melbourne, both with sculpture by Birnie Philip.[94] Other commissions were mostly for ecclesiastical buildings as Scott, as a devout Anglican as well as a missionary for Gothic, was naturally interested in the campaigns to build churches in distant lands with very different climates. After all, his grandfather, Thomas Scott, was much involved in the Church Missionary Society, and his mother came from Antigua in the West Indies. For most of these colonial commissions, Scott waived his fee and worked '*Pro Deo*'. Early on in his career, Scott had written that he hoped Gothic would develop to allow

> *adaptation to different climates and to the usages of other countries; and, what concerns us most directly, to the varied circumstances of the British colonies . . . Our architecture should everywhere be both* English *and* Christian, *but should have in it that intrinsic principle of life which would admit of its ready adaptation to the climate of the torrid or the frozen zone, to the scorched plantations of Jamaica or the icy rocks of Labrador.*[95]

In 1846 Scott sent a design across the Atlantic for a cathedral to be built at St John's, Newfoundland, and his impressive design for a cruciform church in Early English Gothic was eventually completed, after many vicissitudes, by his sons and grandsons. In 1860 he was asked to send out designs for rebuilding St George's Church in Grahamstown, South Africa, as a cathedral, with a proud west tower and spire, and this project, after a long interval, was eventually completed by John Oldrid Scott. Scott was also involved in New Zealand, having been recommended to the Bishop by the testimony of W. E. Gladstone that he was 'the best ecclesiastical architect in Europe, and therefore the world'.[96] He sent out designs for churches that used a timber frame and roof within stone walls, as a response to local conditions and to withstand the earthquakes which beset that colony. It was therefore unfortunate that it was decided that Christ Church Cathedral, commissioned in 1862, should be built entirely in stone, for this building, completed by Benjamin Mountford, was brought down by the devastating earthquake of 2011.

Scott also sent out a design for a church for Australia, at Muswellbrook, New South Wales, which was built to a revised plan by Horbury Hunt. He was less successful in India, his designs for new Anglican churches in Bombay and Calcutta both being rejected on economic grounds. But his somewhat Ruskinian design for a church, Holy Trinity, in Shanghai, was actually built, in 1868–70. All of these colonial church designs were characteristic of Scott's work in Britain, if with adaptations to local conditions. As Alex Bremner wonders in his survey of mid-Victorian Anglican architecture in the British Empire, *Imperial Gothic*, 'are the Anglican churches designed by George Gilbert Scott in Newfoundland, India, South Africa and Australia . . . any less "British" than those by him in Edinburgh, Yorkshire, Cambridge, or on the Channel Island of Alderney?'[97]

With so many commissions, both secular and ecclesiastical, at home and abroad, the question naturally arises as to how Scott was able to handle such a huge volume of work. David Cole concluded that, in the first half of the 1860s, Scott was at work in 37 out of 42 English counties as well as in Scotland and Wales, and that he was restoring churches in 34 counties. 'Eventually he was to work in every county of England and Wales except Cardigan.'[98] But the stories that suggest Scott was unfamiliar with much of what emanated from the office belie the evidence that he was fully in command of a very efficient organisation. After his death, a former pupil, Ralph Neville, was insistent that

> on all occasions every drawing and every single detail of work in his office went
> through his hands and was submitted to his judgement. People may think with such
> a large business, and a multitude of small as well as large buildings, a great deal of
> work was done in the office which he himself knew very little about; but that is a great
> mistake, and it is a marvel, knowing the amount of work he had to do, how he got
> through what he did.[99]

Unfortunately, almost all the papers and account books which would reveal how the business at 31, later 20, Spring Gardens operated are lost (two cash ledgers survive from the very end of Scott's career, revealing that in 1877 the practice received some forty instalments of fees, totalling £8,289, and the following year fifty instalments totalling £10,464). There are, however, a number of jobs that provide evidence about the way the office worked.

One is the commission for the new buildings on a new site for the University of Glasgow, which was given to Scott, without competition, in 1864, and which has been studied by the architectural and business historian Sam McKinstry, who has analysed what he describes as a 'network of trust'. This involved firms and contacts that Scott had built up during his career. The quantities were prepared by the independent surveyors who worked closely with Scott, John Burlison and John Lee. The university accepted the tender of an English contractor, John Thompson of Peterborough, recommended by Scott, rather than that of a local firm, because it could handle masonry, brickwork, ironmongery and other trades. The clerk of works, a crucial appointment, was chosen by Scott, who selected the German-born William Conradi, who had trained in his office and who he regarded as very practical, in preference to the architect Robert Rowand Anderson, who was much liked by the university and who had earlier acted as clerk of works for Scott's church in Leith. There were no complaints from the client. Professor Allen Thomson, the convener of the building committee (whom Scott would see and have lunch with to discuss the design of the university's Bute Hall only two days before he died), wrote to a newspaper in 1870 that

> I am bound to say that I have ever found Mr Scott ready to listen to every suggestion, and to give it effect if, after due consideration, it met with his approval; and I must add that during a continued intercourse by correspondence and personal interview during six years I have had more and more cause to admire the purity of his taste, the quickness and soundness of his judgement and the promptness and exactness of his business arrangements.[100]

McKinstry writes how:

> At the epicentre of the efficient network of trust which had served the university and so many other clients so well was Scott himself, backed up by his office, manned by a carefully organized staff who on the whole adored, admired and were completely loyal to Scott and his architectural talents and ideals. The office was headed up by key individuals in senior positions whose high competence and dedication could be especially relied on.[101]

These included Burlison and John Drayton Wyatt; Richard Coad, another chief assistant; and John Bignold, 'a mine of information on building construction whose soul was wrapped up in the office'.[102] (Wyatt, who had executed so many fine drawings and perspectives for Scott, left the office in 1867 to set up on his own, and asked Scott if he could take on the restoration of Gloucester Cathedral; Scott said no, replying that he had 'been reviewing my position and feel that I must make some radical change on account of my two sons establishing themselves in practice. It is clear that they have a natural claim upon such work.'[103]) Also important were the clerks of works, such as Conradi, James Frater, John Chapple and, above all, the Shetland-born antiquary and architect James Thomas Irvine, who became close to Scott and his architect sons. Then there were the pupils and architectural assistants who had been drawn to Scott's office, many of whom went on to become leading and distinguished architects themselves: Bodley, Street and William White in the early days, later Herbert Austin, Charles Buckeridge, Somers Clarke junior, W. H. Crossland, Thomas Garner, Jackson, R. J. Johnson, Micklethwaite, John Norton, E. R. Robson, J. J. Stevenson and W. S. Weatherley among others. (Articled pupils certainly had to pay for the privilege of being in this celebrated office: the premium was as much as three hundred guineas.) The efficiency as well as the talent of Scott's office in the 1860s was confirmed by the architectural carver, Harry Hems, who had worked on the Foreign Office and who, much later, wrote that,

Scott's success was partly the result of his being in the right place at the right time, but it also owed much to his prodigious capacity for work. McKinstry suggests that his character and behaviour seem to exemplify Max Weber's theories about the debt of capitalism to the Protestant work ethic. This might well be seen in his unremitting hard work and consciousness of the preciousness of time, never wasting a moment to write or draw, particularly during the many hours he spent in railway carriages, as well as in his charismatic leadership and in his discreet benevolence and charity; though in this last he was surely responding to his Christian duty ('when thou doest alms, let not thy left hand know what thy right hand doeth'). He supported several charities and hospitals, in addition to the Architects' Benevolent Fund (in 1870, for instance, it was reported that, in the case of 'the poor woman' who had lost both husband and son and was in court for a debt of eleven shillings after being unable to pay a cab fare, 'The magistrate also received £2 from Mr and Mrs G. G. Scott'[105]).

Scott spent little money on himself and was clearly a driven man, perhaps in reaction to the success of his brothers, four of whom went to Cambridge University and found careers in the Church. He was certainly conscious of his failure to achieve any academic success, and felt that he had wasted much of his early years ('. . . if with the same means of education my brother carried off in his freshman's year one of the highest university classical scholarships, why should not I have been a fair classic?'). Scott had something to prove, and it must have hurt when, having decided to pursue architecture and a family friend told him that 'I have no doubt you will rise to the head of your profession', his

BELOW: Scott's design for the new Royal Courts of Justice: woodcut from *The Builder*, 1867.

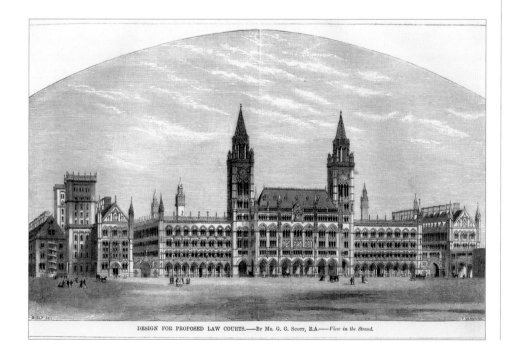

DESIGN FOR PROPOSED LAW COURTS.——By Mr. G. G. Scott, R.A.——*View in the Strand.*

OPPOSITE: Scott's perspective
of an internal corridor in his
unsuccessful competition
entry in the Law Courts
competition 1866.

father at once replied, 'Oh no, his abilities are not sufficient for that', for he recorded this exchange in his *Recollections*. Furthermore (also corresponding to the Weber model), Scott's profound religious faith tended towards a belief in predestination. He wrote of his early success in architecture, 'for which I have to thank a gracious Providence, and without which I really do not know what course I could have taken'. When he was 'awakened from my slumbers by the thunder of Pugin's writings' and 'every aspiration of my heart had become mediaeval', he later 'thought that my experience, and that of some, perhaps many, others pointed to a special interposition of Providence for a special purpose'. And Scott's strong sense of personal calling is clear from his reaction to his clash with Palmerston over the Foreign Office, for, 'To resign would be to give up a sort of property which Providence had placed in the hands of my family.'

There are many testimonies to the amiability and kindness of Scott's character. He was unpretentious, happier in the company of the clergy and his peers than in aristocratic society. He was not smart, either in manner or appearance. All this is clear from T. G. Jackson's revealing recollection of his first meeting with Scott, prior to entering the office in Spring Gardens in 1858.

> I went to breakfast with him and he offered to take me to the 'Brompton Boilers', as the irreverent had christened the temporary buildings in which the South Kensington Museum had its origin . . . We walked . . . till we took an omnibus, from the top of which I remember he disparaged Decimus Burton's arch opposite Apsley House as 'a thing one could design in ten minutes'. In his disregard of personal appearances I think he outmatched my father. His negligent dress and ill-brushed hat were counterbalanced by a certain unconscious dignity in his manner and were part of the modesty and simplicity of the man. He would stand still in the middle of the road and take out a case of pencils and a notebook and illustrate by a sketch what he was saying. I was much touched by the freedom and absence of pretension with which he discussed architecture with me, a mere tyro and a youngster with the merest smattering of knowledge on the subject.[106]

Ewan Christian, consulting architect to the Church Commissioners, with whom he had worked on setting up the Architectural Museum, noted how Scott was ready to meet classes of working men there, and how, on one occasion, 'Sir Gilbert devoted the whole afternoon to shewing those men everything to be seen of value in the Museum, and the kind way, and the laborious way, in which he did it was delightful to see. It was highly appreciated by the men.'[107] And E. W. Godwin recalled that

> he was ever courteous, kindly and pleasant. Always ready to acknowledge earnestly and gracefully the artistic powers of other architects . . . He was one of those who spoke well of you behind your back, and, above all, one who, though he desired to be just in his estimate of men, could look kindly upon their shortcomings . . . It was this 'gentil' courtesy that secured Scott in the good opinion of those he served, and which was one of the main things on which his success depended.[108]

As for the office itself, we also have Jackson's evocative description of it, which deserves reprinting in full.

> Scott's office was a very large one. Counting pupils, salaried assistants, and clerks, I think we were twenty-seven in all. I was put to work in the first-floor room at the

back with six others; there were about a dozen more in two rooms on the second floor; the ground-floor front room, which served also as the waiting-room, was the sanctum of Mr Burlison, the head man, who made the estimates and surveys. Scott's own room was the ground-floor back, and farther back still were the writing clerks and the office-boys. The front room first floor was let to a Mr Moriarty, a barrister, a mysterious person whom we never saw. Of Scott we saw but little. He was up to his eyes in engagements and it was hard to get him to look at our work. I have seen three or four men with drawings awaiting correction or approval grouped outside his door. The door flew open and out he came: 'No time today!'; the cab was at the door and he was whirled away to some cathedral where he would spend a couple of hours and then fly off again to some other great work at the other end of the kingdom. Now and then the only chance of getting instructions was to go with him in a cab to the station . . . It need hardly be said that it is an impossibility really to direct so large a staff as Scott's; but the work had to be done somehow. The heads of different rooms were capable men with a good knowledge of construction; Scott had a wonderful power of making rapid expressive sketches and from these his men were able to produce work which, curiously enough, did fall into something of a consistent style that passed for Gilbert Scott's . . .

Perhaps what did us as much good as anything in Scott's office was the sharp fire of criticism that went on and from which none escaped. Even our master's work fared badly, for the pupils never ran in the regular office grooves like the assistants, and often when sketches came up for some new 'job' we fell upon them and metaphorically tore them to pieces. The salaried assistants, in Scott's absence, were our great resource, and though they used to complain that it was not their business to teach the pupils, they were very good to us.

After mentioning in particular Coad, Bignold and Irvine, Jackson continued:

Of the other assistants I have no very clear recollection except of one whose attendance was somewhat irregular, but who had some secret clue to Scott's movements and was as good as a barometer is for telling the weather, for his appearance at the office was a sure signal of Scott's approach.[109]

With this constant work and incessant travelling, Mrs Scott can have seen little of her workaholic husband except when they went on the occasional holiday together. Caroline would have seen even less of him after the family moved out of London, first to Ham and then to rural Surrey. This is clear from the outpouring of grief and guilt that followed her sudden death, on 24 February 1872, after some years of ill health with heart disease.

How did I, and do I still, blame myself for a thousand little things I might have done but did not think to do! How many things I might have said but did not think to say! Oh! If I could have but one year more of her dear companionship, how much more affectionate, considerate, kind and studious of her happiness would I be! But oh! It is now too late – Oh! Lord forgive my thoughtlessness, my ignorance and my negligences! Oh my dearest wife, if thou canst hear me now forgive the faults which thou knowest but too well!

And again,

Oh! That I had appreciated the danger of these attacks and had taken more precautions. Oh! – that I had taken occasion from then to be more demonstrative in my affection to have been more tender and considerate and to have more carefully avoided my natural fretfulness and irritability and watched every opportunity of showing my love! How sadly and bitterly I repent having got into the way of behaving to the dear companion of my life in a matter of course manner of not restraining in her presence as I should in that of people I cared nothing, for the peevishness and impatience of my temper . . .

And it was all due to Scott's frenetic activity. 'My practice took me much from home, and she led a comparatively solitary life. Her great relaxation was when we went to the sea-side, which we did every year, unless some other tour to Wales or to the Lakes engaged us.' Otherwise, as Scott now recognised,

she was so much alone, owing to my best hours being at business and on journeys that I have no doubt she frequently did feel melancholy and when I returned home jaded with work and often disturbed by severe anxiety and disappointment I fear I did little to enliven her spirits.

Scott now realised that he owed much of his success to his late wife.

Her loss to me is that of one of the wisest and best of earthly companions, helpers and advisers . . . She has, over and over again, given me advice of the greatest importance in my profession; she was the means of terminating . . . my partnership with Mr Moffatt, for while I hesitated and delayed, she took the matter into her own hands … My wife was ever an admirable helper to me in my business, always ready with wise advice and encouragement.

DESIGN SUBMITTED FOR THE NEW LAW COURTS, LONDON.
CENTRAL HALL.

ABOVE: John Oldrid Scott's drawing of the domed central hall in his father's design for the Law Courts, as illustrated in Scott's lectures on Medieval architecture published in 1879.

Clearly Caroline was good with money; Scott noted that, 'My dearest wife had a nice income of her own, which I did not interfere with but left at her own entire disposal. She paid out of it, however, a great deal that I ought to have borne, besides exercising much charity.' Many pages of Scott's unpublished *Recollections* were devoted to memories of 'my ever dearest Carry', and to expressions of shame and guilt about his neglect of her. In atonement, he designed a splendid, richly carved monument, of white marble and granite, over her grave in Tandridge churchyard in Surrey. Later, he published the family prayers and devotions Caroline had composed, dedicating the volume to the loved memory of 'the dear companion of the best years of his life, his surest guide, his wisest counsellor, and the sharer of all his joys and sorrows . . . as the best monument to her piety and virtues'.[110]

His wife's death was one of a series of bereavements that Scott had suffered since the middle of the 1860s; several were of siblings, of whom he had seen little since his career took off, which may have suggested to him that his success had come at a price. The worst loss was the death of his third and favourite son, Albert Henry Scott, a gifted boy who had experimented with photography for a while before going up to Exeter College, Oxford, in 1864 (his father seems not to have been interested in exploiting

RIGHT: The entrance to 31, formerly 20, Spring Gardens, Charing Cross, Scott's office from 1838 until his death: a photograph taken for Batsford publishers in c.1911.

FAR RIGHT: The Grove in Hampstead, Scott's home from 1856 until 1864, photographed in 2014.

this new medium for recording his own buildings) (see p. 84).[111] All five sons would appear to have suffered from bouts of ill health, and the move to Ham was made because Hampstead was 'too cold for our younger boys', Alwyne and Dukinfield. Albert was 'far stronger' but, after rowing on the Thames at Ham, he went down with rheumatic fever and died on 30 January 1865. He is buried in Petersham churchyard, under a pink granite tombstone designed by his father.

The series of moves made by Scott and his wife are interesting, and somewhat puzzling. Although by the 1860s he could surely afford to, Scott – unlike Pugin, Street, Waterhouse, Burges and Norman Shaw, among others – did not attempt to design and build a home for himself and his family. They always lived in rented or leased accommodation, usually Georgian houses of a plain character surely inimical to Scott's own taste. At first, Scott and his wife lived above the shop in Spring Gardens, a late eighteenth-century brick terraced house. Here, in 1839, their first child, George Gilbert junior, was born, followed in 1841 by John Oldrid, who would also become an architect. In 1844 the family moved away from this crowded and noisy part of central London to a new house in St John's Wood, 12 Avenue Road (since demolished). Here the other three boys were born: Albert Henry, a few days after the move; Alwyne Gilbert in 1849 and Dukinfield Henry in 1854. The youngest boy was named after his godfather, the Revd Sir Henry Dukinfield, Bt, vicar of St Martin-in-the-Fields, where the Scott family would worship, twice every Sunday, until he resigned the living in 1848. It is known that, when at Avenue Road, the Scotts had a housekeeper, a manservant, three maids, a nanny and a bootboy; they also kept a carriage and pair for Mrs Scott's use.[112]

In 1856 the Scott family moved from St John's Wood up the hill to The Grove at Hampstead, later renamed the Admiral's House, a building once painted by John Constable which now carries a plaque recording Scott's residence. In 1864 came the move to Ham. Scott rented the Manor House, a large early eighteenth-century brick mansion. While living there, Caroline Scott became close to her neighbour at Ham House, Lady Huntingtower, the much-injured and estranged Irish Roman Catholic wife of the cruel and dissolute younger son of the Earl of Dysart. But just five years later, the family moved again, renting Parkhurst, a mid-Georgian house near Leith Hill in Surrey (which no longer stands). This cannot have been satisfactory – it was over five miles from the nearest railway station – for the following year, in 1870, Scott moved to Rook's Nest, a large country house in extensive grounds below the North Downs near Godstone. Scott described this as 'a charming residence' but it is, in fact, a rather gaunt symmetrical seven-bay, two-storey Georgian house (altered earlier in the century by John Shaw, who possibly added the Ionic porch). This seems an unlikely home for a busy church architect and ardent Goth: perhaps Scott took these large houses and lived in grand style to please Caroline. On the night of the 1871 Census it is recorded that Scott was at home with his wife and two of their five sons (Dukinfield and Alwyne), his valet, 'my good servant' John Pavings and no fewer than nine domestic servants (eight of them female); they also employed two gardeners and a coachman.

In 1870, while residing at Rook's Nest, Scott declined to be nominated by the Council of RIBA to stand as President, 'feeling that my extensive engagements, my distance from London, and the claims of my family upon my spare time forbade it. I felt also that I was not, by nature fitted for such a post' (T. H. Wyatt was chosen, but Scott accepted the nomination three years later). Rook's Nest was easier to reach than Parkhurst, but Scott still had some distance to travel every day. He presumably came home from London by train on the London, Brighton and South Coast Railway's branch to Caterham, which had opened in 1856, and then by taking a fly or his own carriage for the last three miles. But, even allowing for the efficiency of the Victorian railway system, Scott must at first have spent little time in the house, except on Sundays. Later that year, in October, Scott suffered a heart attack at Chester and was seriously ill, unable to return home for five weeks. After that, he must have convalesced at Godstone for some months. His life was becoming overshadowed by illness and death: he later found that Caroline had recorded, at Christmas in 1871 two months before she died, that: 'Gilbert tells me tonight Dr H(ayman) did not think he would live when he was so ill at Eastbourne – and John has been almost as ill and who can tell what may occur – and oh when I am gone and Dear G(eorge) may not live very long – who will pray for them – who will ask God's tender mercy for them.'

Rook's Nest was the residential apogee of Scott's social ascent. After his illness and Caroline's death in 1872, Scott began to scale down his practice and activity; he also retreated back to Ham in 1873, sharing the Manor House with the younger boys and John Oldrid and his wife, Mary Anne, the daughter of his friend the Revd Thomas Stevens, the founder of Bradfield College (for which he had designed buildings). And then, in 1876, prompted by increasing ill health, he returned to London. In his *Recollections*, Scott wrote how,

During the autumn [of 1875] I became painfully impressed in the costliness of my mode of living and the falling off of my practice – and as my son and daughter in law did not care for Ham, determined to remove to London whether wisely or not God knows! We did not finally move until a year later – I am now a Londoner and have much lost in position. May God bless the change! I fear it was not quite well considered.

BELOW: The Manor House at Ham, Scott's home in 1864–69 and again in 1872–76.

The fear of loss of social status here is interesting, for Scott was moving from a house in the country to a brand new town house in a new suburban development in Brompton, or South Kensington. He had bought the ninety-nine-year lease of an unremarkable five-storey, yellow-brick and stucco vaguely Classical terraced house on a street corner in Collingham Road on the Gunter Estate. The house overlooked Courtfield Gardens and, to keep up appearances, Scott rather pretentiously called it Courtfield House. At least he could see something Gothic out of his windows, as over the road was the new ragstone church dedicated to St Jude designed by George Godwin. The move may not have been well considered, but Scott remained in Courtfield House with his second son, John Oldrid, and his wife, and his youngest, Dukinfield, and was soon complaining that the local Vestry had failed to pave the Cromwell Road west of Gloucester Road, so that newly built houses (several of which he seems to have owned) remained unlet. And it was in this house that, two years later, he died.

Scott's illness in Chester, no doubt brought on by decades of overwork and constant travel, was very serious. The newspapers reported that he was lying 'dangerously ill at the residence of the Dean of Chester, where he was taken ill as he was passing through the city to Oswestry'.[113] The diagnosis was 'a complication of bronchitis and disease of the heart'. Scott himself recounted how he

> *was threatened with a fatal disease, being suddenly attacked, while at Chester, in the heart and lungs. I was detained at the deanery for five weeks before I could return home: my dear wife went down there to be with me, and she brought me home, and by God's mercy, I was, in the course of the following spring, sufficiently restored to resume my usual engagements. Lord spare me and forgive my great unworthiness and unprofitableness!*

In fact, Scott was unable to resume work for some months, and never fully regained his former health; he was conspicuously absent from public events during 1871 and had to cancel his lectures at the Royal Academy.

ABOVE LEFT: Rook's Nest near Godstone, Surrey, Scott's grandest residence where he and his family lived in 1870–72, photographed in 2011.

ABOVE RIGHT: Scott's final home: 'Courtfield House', a large terraced house in Collingham Road, South Kensington, where he died in 1878. Photograph 2014.

The following year, however, brought an invitation that he could not decline. It was one occasioned by the completion of the Albert Memorial. 'I have been this day to Osborne to be knighted,' he recorded in his *Recollections* on 9 August 1872.

> *I have had a very agreeable day. I was summoned to Osborne to the council, and was invited to go down by special train at nine o'clock . . . We went down together to Gosport, where we adjourned to a large man-of-war's boat of twelve oars, and were rowed, under the command of an officer, to the mouth of the harbour. Here we embarked on a fine steamer, and proceeded towards the Isle of Wight . . . On reaching the house, after a little walking about, I was asked to go with the ministers towards the presence chamber. Among them was Lord Bridport with a sword, which he informed me was to be used on me. We waited on a staircase a long time . . . and while we waited there the Prince of Wales passed through the staircase. He shook hands with and congratulated me . . . [A]t length I was summoned. Having made my bows, the sword was handed to the Queen. She touched both my shoulders with it and said in a familiar gentle way, 'Sir Gilbert.' Then she held out her hand, I kneeled again and kissed it, and backed out, the whole taking something less than a minute . . . We then adjourned to luncheon with some of the ladies and gentlemen of the Court. I had been there once before, and had lunched there then in the same way: this was some nine years ago, when my design for the Prince Consort memorial was first adopted.*

Scott decided to be known by the name Gilbert because: 'My dearest wife would have chosen it as she used to tell me to call myself "Mr Gilbert Scott". I thank God for this honour!'

In 1873 he suffered another attack, 'which led me to make a long stay abroad'. Scott left home in July and was out of the country for the rest of the year, travelling to Germany, Switzerland, France and Italy, staying for five weeks with his old friend J. H. Parker in Rome. The following year Scott took another extended trip abroad; clearly the once-busy architect was now taking it easier. Scott's youngest brother, the Revd Melville Horne Scott, later suffered from similar heart problems and suggested that the condition was hereditary.

¼ Ross. A.G.S.   ¼ Ross: D. H. S.

ABOVE LEFT: Scott's wife, Caroline Oldrid, and their second son, John Oldrid Scott, photographed in the early 1860s by their third son Albert Henry Scott.

ABOVE CENTRE: Scott's fourth son, Alwyn Gilbert Scott, photographed by his brother Albert.

ABOVE RIGHT: Scott's youngest son, Dukinfield Henry Scott, photographed by his brother Albert.

Do the doctors not think that I do not know what the pain in my left arm means? It is the angina, from which my father died; I can remember the pulling of the bell as if it were yesterday. My brothers John and Samuel both died of it. Gilbert had it, and he would start with the pain as he wrote his letters, and then write on in spite of it.[114]

When Scott was incapacitated, the responsibility for running the office was taken over by his architect sons, who may not have relished the task. Indeed, after 1871 the office was slowly reduced in size as fewer new commissions came in. There is also a perceptible decline in the quality of the work. The church of St Mary Abbots in Kensington, for instance, is large and imposing, expensively fitted out, but somehow formulaic and in its details dull. This important commission was eventually completed by John Oldrid Scott, upon whom Scott increasingly relied. St Paul's in New Southgate, a ragstone church of 1873, might have been designed two decades earlier. All Souls, or the Hook Memorial Church, in Leeds, begun in 1876, is, however, a sophisticatedly severe and impressive building – although it is, of course, impossible to know who was actually responsible for the design. The finest of Scott's last churches is that at Fulney, near Spalding, completed posthumously by J. O. Scott, which has most unusual and inventive arcades.

What is clear is that Scott began increasingly to collaborate with his second son. In 1872 he was invited to enter the (first) competition for a parliament house in Berlin following the unification of Germany under Prussia, and together they submitted a design which incorporated Scott's resourceful ideas for a Gothic dome, a structure without precedent in Britain, which he had first developed in his Law Courts competition design (see p. 86). Scott admitted that

the noblest of all forms by which a space can be covered is the dome; and, much more than this, that of all architectural forms it is the most sublime and the most poetic, and is susceptible of, and demands, the highest artistic treatment. I deplore, therefore, its non-existence in our old English architecture.[115]

However, he was no more successful in raising a Gothic dome in Berlin than he had been in London, and it was left to F. W. Stevens to realise the concept in his Victoria Terminus in Bombay (a building much influenced by St Pancras), as well as to Imre Steindl with the Hungarian parliament building in Budapest.

Scott was more successful in the limited competition for St Mary's Episcopal Cathedral in Edinburgh, announced the same year. Possibly owing to the strong support of the new Bishop, his design was preferred to those submitted by Street, Burges and three Scottish architects. The result is a scholarly pile rising unexpectedly from the surrounding grey Classical terraces. Details from several Medieval Scottish buildings were developed to create a noble structure, although the three stone spires which add to the skyline of the Scottish capital were surely inspired by Lichfield. Only the nave was completed before Scott's death, and it was left to John Oldrid Scott and *his* architect son to complete the cathedral to the original design. It must be said that neither this grand cathedral nor most of the many churches Scott designed during his long career approach in vigour, splendour or interest the towering church with its tall spire that he had designed for Hamburg back in the 1840s.

Although commissions for new churches began to decline, Scott continued to be much involved in cathedral restoration, even taking on new ones: Rochester, Exeter and Canterbury – the refurnishing of the choirs in the latter two provoking some controversy. At Exeter, where he had to battle constantly with the Dean, he was criticised for wanting to *retain* the ancient choir screen, and then his new reredos was threatened with removal by a petition from the Chancellor of the Diocese, W. J. Phillpotts, because of its sculptured imagery. The reredos was declared illegal by the Bishop in 1874 under old church law, but was eventually reprieved by the Judicial Committee of the Privy Council. As Scott put it, 'the injunctions of the sixteenth century were at first directed against such imagery as had been abused for superstitious purposes . . . and therefore could not be applied to new sculpture intended for no such purposes'. *The Spectator* observed after this once-celebrated case that, 'We might possibly find an Englishman or two capable of worshipping a steam-engine or a telegraph with a superstitious worship, but not one anywhere capable of feeling the like sentiment towards a statue.'[116] (See p. 87.) But there is a certain irony in the fact that Scott, who was far from High Church and who, according to his eldest son, was opposed to Roman Catholic practices 'principally upon the use of images which he could not but think was *almost* if not quite idolatrous', should have been responsible for work condemned as popish by Low Church Protestants.

Scott agreed to serve as President of RIBA, for three years, in 1873. His presidential speech – delivered in November when he was abroad by Charles Eastlake – was pessimistic and defensive in tone, suggesting the disillusionment of an ageing and ill man. After referring to earlier periods and to the more recent 'revived feeling for the study and resuscitation of Mediaeval architecture' with which he had been so much involved, he confessed that he felt that 'until we can resuscitate among ourselves a glorious enthusiasm, like to that which has in former times given rise to the great movements in our art, it is vain to hope for another great period in architecture'. Scott then lamented that:

The million ugly houses, or even the majority of them, may go to decay, or be rebuilt; but a single ancient edifice destroyed or ruined by ignorant 'restoration,' can never be recovered . . . Our old buildings, too often – nay, in a majority, I fear, of cases – fall into the hands of men who have neither knowledge nor respect for them, while, even among those who possess the requisite knowledge, there has too often been a lack of

ABOVE: A perspective of the unsuccessful entry submitted by Scott and his second architect son in the competition for the Imperial German Parliament in Berlin announced in 1872.

veneration, a disposition to sit in judgement on the work of their teachers, a rage for alteration to suit some system to which they had pledged themselves in their own works; and even the preposterous idea that the ancient examples they were called on to repair were a fitting field for the display of their own originality!

The ever-topical subject of church restoration was much on his mind, and he deplored the fact that

our country has actually been robbed of a large proportion of its antiquities under the name of 'restoration;' and the work of destruction and spoliation still goes on merrily; while, at the public festivities by which each auto-da-fé *is celebrated, we find ecclesiastical dignitaries, clergy, squires and architects congratulating one another on the success of the latest effort of Vandalism.[117]*

The increasingly acrimonious controversy over restoration would dog Scott's presidency. In its second year, 1874, John Ruskin declined the award of the Royal Gold Medal on the grounds that the Institute had not done enough to protect ancient buildings from destruction and damage, not only in England but also, and more so, in Italy. In a private letter to Scott he also explained that whereas he would once have been happy to accept a medal, he now felt that the professionalisation of architecture lay behind much bad restoration practice and that he was increasingly worried about the direction in which the Institute was going.

The Primary object of all such Associations is to exalt the power of their own Profession over the mind of the public, power being – in the present century synonymous with Wealth. And the root of all the evil and ruin which this century has seen . . . is summed up in four words 'Commission on the Cost'.[118]

FAR LEFT: The Gothic dome
Scott proposed for Berlin
as drawn by F. E. Jones and
illustrated in Scott's lectures
on Mediaeval architecture.

LEFT: Scott's controversial
design for a new reredos
in Exeter Cathedral:
a woodcut published in
The Builder in 1874.

Scott took this rebuff personally, as well he might, for as the best-known and most prolific of church and cathedral restorers he was widely regarded as representative of the practice and, for some, the most culpable. Naturally, he devoted his opening address that year to the subject, and, while defending the Institute, admitted that much deliberate destruction of ancient buildings was still going on.

> *We may, on the one hand, very fairly protest against the injustice of being made in any degree responsible for acts in which we have had no hand, over which we had no control, and against which we should protest as loudly as Mr Ruskin: but on the other hand, we, being the incorporated representatives of architectural practice, may, in a certain sense, be held to represent its vices as well as its virtues, and in the eyes of a self-constituted censor, and one who from his first appearance before the public has devoted himself wholly to protest and warning, we can hardly wonder that, if he holds us responsible, he should not think it a time for us to be playing at compliments with our censor . . . To Mr Ruskin's eye the best of our restorations are mere vandalisms, for he protests against them root and branch.[119]*

(Elsewhere, Scott claimed that he had spoken out against 'the modern system of radical restoration' which was 'doing more towards the destruction of ancient art than the ravings of fanaticism' some eight years earlier than Ruskin's celebrated denunciation of restoration in *The Seven Lamps of Architecture* in 1849, that, 'It means the most total destruction which a building can suffer'). Scott returned to the subject in his third annual address in 1875, stressing the importance of making accurate records of 'perishing architectural remains', and while admitting that the majority of old churches 'are almost utterly despoiled, and nine-tenths, if not all, of their interest swept away . . . Yet, happily, a remnant remains: a few churches in each district are still left unrestored; and for the preservation of these, like the remnant of the Sibylline books, it is worth while to pay any price.'[120]

Worse was to come. In 1877 Scott was subject to a number of personal attacks over his restoration practice. First, in March, came William Morris's letter to the *Athenaeum*, provoked by Scott's restoration of Tewkesbury Abbey, which advocated 'an association for the purpose of watching over and protecting these relics', the result being the foundation of the Society for the Protection of Ancient Buildings, or 'The Anti-Scrape', soon after. Scott responded by complaining to a friend that 'I do not deserve it, I never seek to see these articles, much less to answer them'. In truth, of course, Scott always responded to criticism by defending himself at length. This time he again pointed out that

> *I have lifted up my voice on this subject for more than thirty years, and though not faultless, have striven with all my might to avoid such errors, and to prevent their commission by others. I feel more deeply on this subject than any other, and never lose an opportunity of protesting against barbarisms of this kind, in season and out of season. I am, therefore, willing to be sacrificed by being made the victim in a cause which I have so intensely at heart.*

In June came a long article on 'Thorough Restoration' by the Revd W. J. Loftie in *Macmillan's Magazine*. This was not the first time Scott's restorations had been attacked by this Ulster-born antiquary and prolific author, who was then assistant chaplain at the Savoy Chapel in London, and, as Scott noted in his *Recollections*, 'He seems irrepressible, for no matter how often a statement of his is refuted, he reiterates it just as if no such refutation had been made. Happily he is an Irishman, and his own bulls are his best refutation.' Naturally Scott soon penned a reply, which was published in the July number of the same magazine under the title 'Thorough Anti-Restoration'.

But the most devastating attack was the lecture delivered at RIBA in May – with Scott in the audience – by his former assistant, the Glaswegian architect J. J. Stevenson. Entitled 'Architectural Restoration: Its Principles and Practice', this was much more damaging as it was much better informed. Stevenson pointed out that it was all very well for architects to condemn destructive restoration, and for the Institute to issue advice on the subject, but there was a profound discordance between ideal principles and actual practice. He condemned the conventional prejudice against Perpendicular Gothic, but went further. Responding as he was in his own architectural work to the contemporary revival of interest in Classical architecture, Stevenson was particularly scathing about the widespread and almost automatic destruction of Post-Reformation furnishings – something of which Scott had certainly been guilty. As a Scots Presbyterian, Stevenson clearly had no sympathy with High Church ecclesiology, and he attacked

> *the view which seems to be held by all restorers, from the most eminent, learned and conservative to the most ignorant and destructive, that the Reformation was a mistake; that since then the Church of England has no history worth recording; and that the historical monuments, and the ecclesiastical arrangements of these three centuries of darkness and degradation, ought to be destroyed. This, we know, has been the almost universal practice in restorations.*[121]

Scott responded to this 'kindly cruelty' immediately after the lecture and then, on 11 June, delivered a long lecture of his own in reply. Yet again he went over his long history as a restorer and as an opponent of excessive restoration, both accepting the justice of some criticisms and refuting others, pointing out that so often the destruction of such things as seventeenth-century woodwork was due to clients and patrons, and also that, when faced with a neglected and often structurally unsound Medieval building, doing nothing was not an option. 'I could also wish myself that the 'do-nothing' system could be applied to old buildings, if only as an experiment; but I fear it would meet with the same fate as when proposed to human patients.' And Scott began his paper, with wit as well as justice, by asking,

> *Why* I – *who have laid myself out to protest against the havoc which has been made through the length and breadth of the land under the name of Restoration – should be singled out as the special butt of this yet stronger protest, it is not easy to say. In accepting this challenge, I may claim a somewhat back-handed compliment. When Napoleon III was told that a prophetic authority had pronounced him to be Anti-Christ, he replied, 'He does me too much honour!' Much the same is the honour intended to be conferred on me.*

All these necessary and pertinent criticisms of the practice of church restoration, which had been such good business for architects for the preceding four decades, clearly hurt Scott as they were so often personal in character. Much of the fifth and last manuscript volume of his *Recollections* was devoted to the restoration debate: a defence, entitled 'The Anti-Restoration Movement', was written in October 1877, and more was written in November in response to an article on 'Restoration and anti-restoration' by Sidney Colvin, a founder member of SPAB, which had been published in *The Nineteenth Century* the previous month. It is surely significant that Scott's eldest son, who was increasingly sympathetic to the Anti-Scrape cause, nevertheless published his father's ripostes to both Stevenson and Loftie as an appendix in the published volume of *Recollections*.

Scott's very last piece of writing was not about church restoration, however, but about an architectural development which caused him some distress as it represented an abandonment of the crusade for the Gothic, of the belief that the style was modern and could be universal, which had dominated his professional life. Dated January 1878, it was a short critical essay about 'The "Queen Anne" Style', 'a vexatious disturber of the Gothic movement'. In this, Scott recounted his commitment to the Gothic cause after being awakened 'by the thunder of Pugin's writings', and then how the course of the Gothic Revival

OPPOSITE: St Mary's Homes at Godstone, ostensibly designed by Scott in 1872 but more likely the work of one of his two architect sons, photographed in 2011.

Sir Gilbert Scott. R.A.
June 27. 1877.

Geo. Richmond

was first disturbed by the Italian mania, arising from Mr Ruskin's writings; then by the French rage, coming in with the Lille Cathedral competition; and later on by the revulsion against this, which might have set things right again, had not many who had been most ardently French – so much so that no moderate man could hold his own for their gallomania – became as furiously anti-gothic; and to carry out their views turned round in favour of seventeenth-century work, and finally of 'Queen Anne.'

Now Scott found that this new, eclectic, free-Classical style – 'half-way between gothic and classic in its effect' – had not only been taken up by a younger generation of architects like J. J. Stevenson, but even by his own architect sons.

Scott admitted that 'so far the change has been an unquestionable gain: we have rich colour and lively, picturesque architecture in lieu of the dull monotony of the usual street architecture', and the style also 'has the advantage of eluding the popular objections to gothic, when used for secular purposes'. But Scott, committed to a modern Gothic and to using new materials as he was, clearly found it baffling that 'the Queen Anne-ites soon . . . freely adopted lead lights, iron casements, and all kinds of old fashions which a gothic architect would have hardly dared to employ, so much so, indeed, that a so-called "Queen Anne" house is now more a revival of the past than a modern gothic house'. Which suggests that St Mary's Homes at Godstone near Rook's Nest, a charming group of half-timbered almshouses with leaded-light windows built in 1872 and attributed to the famous widower who had lived nearby at Rook's Nest, is much more likely to be the work of George Gilbert Scott junior or John Oldrid Scott. Even so, Scott seems to have been anxious to keep up with architectural fashion; his Savernake cottage hospital near Marlborough of 1871–72 was designed in tile-hung 'domestic Gothic' reminiscent of the work of Norman Shaw. In 1876 he made his last trip abroad, to Germany, in connection with the revival of the project to build a new Rathaus in Hamburg. He prepared an extraordinary design, on the lines of his earlier, 1855 project with a central tower, but with Early Renaissance rather than Gothic detail. However, despite the influence of his friend Reichensperger, Scott found himself debarred from this second competition as he was a foreigner.

There was one last literary endeavour with which Scott was concerned in these last years, which was preparing the lectures he had delivered intermittently between 1857 and 1873 at the Royal Academy of Arts. He had been elected an Associate of the Academy in 1855, became a full Academician in 1860 and was appointed Professor of Architecture in 1868. These eighteen lectures 'were written with much zeal; and thanks to my staff, and to my pupils, my sons, and others, they were magnificently and profusely illustrated; more so, perhaps, than any such Lectures had ever been before', he characteristically added. They were published posthumously, in two volumes, with illustrations drawn by 'my friend and assistant' W. S. Weatherley, as *Lectures on the Rise and Development of Mediaeval Architecture delivered at the Royal Academy.*

Scott's preface to this work was dated February 1878, when he was still active, giving a lecture in Leeds and visiting the works at Tewkesbury. He continued to be busy but began suddenly to decline towards the end of the following month, suffering from varicose veins in one leg and from rheumatism. One of his last acts was to write out a cheque for a Roman Catholic architect 'who had had great misfortunes and was lying ill'. Scott's faithful valet, John Pavings, disapproved, but he replied that, 'It is very wicked to speak harshly of poor people.' George Gilbert Scott died in the early morning of Wednesday, 27 March, 1878. He was sixty-six years old.

ABOVE: George Gilbert Scott junior and his wife Ellen King Sampson in 'Queen Anne' dress, a *carte-de-visite* photograph by W. M. Clarke taken in their Hampstead garden, probably in c.1872.

OPPOSITE: Sir Gilbert Scott as sketched by George Richmond in 1877 as a study for the Presidential portrait for the Royal Institute of British Architects.

EPILOGUE

It was at the immediate request of both the Dean of Westminster and the Royal Institute of British Architects that, ten days later, Sir Gilbert Scott was buried in Westminster Abbey rather than in Surrey, next to his wife, in Tandridge churchyard. His grave, not far from that of Sir Charles Barry on the north side of the nave near to a new pulpit he had designed (since removed), was covered by a brass designed by his old pupil, G. E. Street, in 1881. Scott made a last will in 1876. This provided for a number of legacies, including one to John Pavings, and for the paying off of loans made to members of his wider family. After settling mortgages and debts, the residue was to be divided equally between his four surviving sons. It is possible that Scott did not realise quite how much he was worth, for in the event his estate amounted to about £120,000 – a huge sum by contemporary standards – leaving those sons very comfortably off.

One son, the fourth, only outlived his father by eight months. Alwyne (or Alwyn) Gilbert Scott went up to Christ Church, Oxford in 1868 and trained as a barrister, being called to the Bar at the Inner Temple in 1876. He died in November 1878, of hepatitis and haematemesis, at his home, Woodlands, at Remenham near Henley-on-Thames at the age of twenty-nine. Four years later his wife, Harriet Hester, died in the same house. Scott's youngest boy, Dukinfield Henry Scott, also went up to Christ Church, to read classics, but he then trained as an engineer and pursued his interest in botany and palaeobotany. He went on to have a distinguished career in the field, becoming the honorary director of the Jodrell Laboratory at Kew. He married one of his students, Henderina Victoria Klaassen, and died at his home, East Oakley House, near Basingstoke, in 1934.

John Oldrid Scott, the second son, returned to Spring Gardens, his birthplace, as an articled pupil after attending school at Bradfield College. He was close to his father, who in his last years shared both the Manor House at Ham and Courtfield House with him and his wife, Mary Anne. J. O. Scott became increasingly important as an assistant and collaborator, eventually inheriting the practice. In his will, Scott left his architectural books and his practice to be divided between and shared by his two architect sons, who he hoped would enter into partnership. But he must have realised that they were unlikely to work together, as he gave J. O. Scott 'the option of taking the said messuage and premises No. 31 Spring Gardens and the said office furniture effects and

chattels and declare that he alone shall have the custody of my business papers and documents'.[122] This option J. O. Scott took, continuing with a number of large, incomplete projects including St Mary Abbots, Edinburgh Episcopal Cathedral and the restoration of Selby Abbey. Although the office continued, run by Charles Baker King, a number of long-serving assistants soon left, and J. O. Scott clearly did not want to preside over a large practice, writing to J. T. Irvine soon after his father's death that,

> *Gilbert and I intend working together like twins for the completion of the works in hand. As regards further works we have agreed to settle nothing at present. Neither of us is anxious to have a great business at any time and it may suit our health and happiness better to work apart when the present things are done.*

Within two years, J. O. Scott had begun to dispose of many of the accumulated drawings and papers built up over four decades, including early letters between his parents, writing to J. T. Irvine that, 'The quantity is so enormous that it was quite necessary to thin them down.'[123] Irvine – who annotated this letter 'Pulping of Sir G. G. Scott's general drawings!!' – rescued some of the sketchbooks and drawings of his revered old boss, which were eventually given to the Bodleian Library at Oxford, only to be disposed of as salvage during the Second World War. The reputation of J. O. Scott has long been overshadowed by those of his father and elder brother, so it should be said that he was a good architect and a careful restorer in his own right, refusing to be bullied by Lord Grimthorpe over the west front of St Albans Abbey. Perhaps his finest work was the Greek Orthodox cathedral of St Sophia in Bayswater of 1877, which was not Gothic but a pioneering essay in the Byzantine Revival. After his father's death, he lived first at Blunt House in Croydon and then in the house he designed for himself near Oxted in Surrey. He died in 1913, his practice being continued by his son, Charles Marriott Oldrid Scott.

Scott's eldest son had already emerged as a sophisticated and influential architect by 1878, but his later life was tragic, and scandalous. George Gilbert Scott junior was unusually talented. He won a scholarship to Eton and then, after serving his articles at Spring Gardens, became an undergraduate at Jesus College, Cambridge, graduating head of the Moral Sciences Tripos in 1866. Two years later he won the Burney

Prize for a philosophical, theological essay and was eventually elected a Fellow of the college, which he was obliged soon to relinquish because of his marriage to Ellen King Sampson in 1872 (at this time, dons were still required to be celibate). It was as if Scott's own academic ambitions were realised through his brilliant eldest son. Scott junior also shared archaeological and antiquarian interests with his father, working with him on a number of restoration projects as well as assisting with several jobs in Cambridge. But the relationship with his father must have been uneasy as Scott junior was close to the Morris circle in the 1860s, even designing a wallpaper for the firm. He also designed a number of vicarages and houses in the new 'Queen Anne' style his father lamented and then, in 1874, caused controversy with his design for St Agnes, Kennington, south London, by looking to the despised Perpendicular for inspiration.

If there was tension between the younger Scott and other members of his family, it was largely owing to religion. He was drawn to the Anglo-Catholic wing of the Church of England, but he waited until after his father's death before going over to Rome. This perversion caused a breach with, in particular, his younger architect brother. In 1881, Scott junior wrote to Irvine that he had not

> had the cold shoulder given me anywhere, except that my own brother John has refused me his house, and has kicked me out of Spring Gardens, which although he is letting off the greater part of the old house to strangers, he will not permit me to use, even as a mere business address. For fear, as he does not hesitate to tell me right out, it might injure his own pecuniary prospects with the deans and dignitaries of the established church. This is surely a pity.[124]

But he was not to find peace of mind. After publishing his scholarly *Essay on the History of English Church Architecture* in 1881, Scott junior's behaviour became increasingly erratic, deluded and violent, exacerbated by drinking, such that in 1883 he had to be confined in the Bethlem Hospital in Lambeth (like poor Pugin three decades before). But he soon escaped, and travelled across the Channel to Rouen, where, it emerged, he had a French mistress.

The situation for Scott's wife Ellen was intolerable as, with five young children, she had no access to her frequently violent husband's considerable wealth. The result was that,

in 1884, Scott junior was subjected to a public inquisition at Lincoln's Inn under the 1862 Lunacy Act, and was found to be of unsound mind and incapable of managing himself or his affairs. He was nevertheless still able to design, and continued with the large Roman Catholic church (today a cathedral) in Norwich he was building for the Duke of Norfolk. But manic-depressive and violent incidents continued, and he was confined in St Andrew's Hospital, Northampton (where the chapel was a work by his father, embellished by his brother), in 1888 and again in 1891–92. George Gilbert Scott junior died of heart disease, cirrhosis of the liver and exhaustion in May 1897 in one of Sir Gilbert Scott's most celebrated and prominent buildings, the Midland Grand Hotel at St Pancras, where he seems to have been placed as a long-term resident by the Visitors in Lunacy. It was as if, even in death, there was no escape from the shadow of his famous father.

The younger Scott's youngest two sons, Giles and Adrian, also became architects, although they hardly knew their father. Giles Gilbert Scott (1880–1960) sprang to fame by winning the competition for the proposed new Anglican cathedral in Liverpool despite being only twenty-two years old and, worse, a Roman Catholic. He went on to become one of the most resourceful and inspired British architects of the new century, designing churches, university buildings, electricity-generating stations and the GPO telephone kiosk, and was chosen to rebuild the House of Commons, in modern Gothic, after the destruction of the old chamber during the Second World War. Sir Giles Scott had a conventionally dismissive attitude towards the architecture of the previous century, often remarking that, 'Grandfather was the successful practical man, and a phenomenal scholar in Gothic precedent, but Father was the artist.' Very different in temperament, and preferring to run a much smaller office, but, like his grandfather, knighted, and sometime President of RIBA, his success at creating prominent buildings in London, Cambridge, Oxford and elsewhere has led to enduring confusion between two famous and great architects, one of the nineteenth century, one of the twentieth, both known as Sir G. Gilbert Scott, RA.

PART TWO

THE BUILDINGS

SCOTT & MOFFATT

George Gilbert Scott and William Bonython Moffatt were in architectural partnership for a decade, from 1836 until 1846 (although Caroline Scott had wisely initiated the breaking of the partnership the preceding year). It was the desire to secure commissions for the new Union workhouses that had brought the two ambitious and energetic young architects together, and for the first few years they designed little else but these structures. On one count, Scott and Moffatt were responsible for some forty-four workhouses. Many of these hated 'bastilles' for the poor were severely utilitarian in plan and style, but Scott was responsible for some more expensive workhouses in a Tudor or Jacobean manner, often employing decorative contrasts in the colour and texture of building materials as at Amersham. Some of these buildings, having later served as hospitals, have been converted to residential use, but several have been demolished. Other institutional commissions followed the workhouses, notably the Infant Orphan Asylum at Wanstead and Reading Gaol. Scott and Moffatt collaborated on the workhouse projects but when commissions for new churches and restorations began to come to the office in the early 1840s the two architects seem to have worked separately, Scott being much more interested in church work. When the split came, Scott sent round a circular to secure business but found that '"Scott and Moffatt" had become so well known as a *nom-de-guerre*, that it took very many years to get rid of it altogether …'

RIGHT: Amersham: the central block beyond the porter's lodge.
Having been a hospital, this handsome workhouse has been
converted into gated residential accommodation, known as
'Gilbert Scott Court'.

TOWCESTER UNION WORKHOUSE, REAR

LEFT: Towcester Union Workhouse, Northamptonshire, of 1836, photographed in 1991; one of the most grimly utilitarian of Scott & Moffatt's workhouses, since – surprisingly – converted into housing.

AMERSHAM UNION WORKHOUSE

OPPOSITE ABOVE: Amersham Union Workhouse, Buckinghamshire, built in 1838, photographed in 2014. This, along with the one at Windsor, both in the 'Elizabethan style', were among the most expensive and elaborately treated of all the workhouses. Scott wrote how these 'went almost as much too far in this direction, as the earlier ones in meanness'.

OPPOSITE BELOW: Amersham: The gable over the entrance, showing the date of construction and the unusual use of polychromy in red brick and flint.

OUNDLE UNION WORKHOUSE

LEFT: Oundle Union Workhouse, Northamptonshire, of 1836, photographed in 1982 and since demolished; the utilitarian nature of the institution was somewhat humanised by the Classical treatment of the entrance range.

CHURCHES

Although he began with workhouses and would go on to design major public buildings, Scott was first and foremost a church architect. Old Medieval churches were his first love and he was soon anxious to design new ones. Thanks to the Victorian church-building boom resulting from the revival of the Church of England and to his family's clerical connections, church work dominated his practice by the mid-1840s. Most of his new churches followed the Medieval conventions affirmed by the Cambridge Camden Society and the ecclesiological movement, by having a nave with two aisles and a separate chancel. Few were experimental in plan, although some were triple-aisled under separate roofs, some with only a single aisle and a few were single vessels with no arcades. Rather than having a lean-to roof, Scott often gave his aisles a series of transverse gables. A steeple was almost always intended, usually picturesquely sited to the west, but sometimes over the crossing. On the whole, Scott designed for moderate, middle-of-the-road Anglicans. As he famously remarked, 'Amongst Anglican architects, Carpenter and Butterfield were apostles of the high church school – I, of the multitude … [A]s they became the mouth-pieces – or hand-pieces – of the Cambridge Camden Society, while I took an independent course, it followed that they were chiefly employed by men of advanced views, who placed no difficulties in their way, but the reverse; while I, doomed to deal with the promiscuous herd, had to battle over and over again the first prejudices, and had to be content with such success as I could get.' Although Scott occasionally adopted fashionable mannerisms, gave his churches an apse rather than a square east end and was influenced by the taste for French and Italian Gothic, his church work was not as innovative as that by his former pupils Bodley and Street, let alone the assertively original Butterfield. He once wrote that, 'In our church architecture we have, as I consider, little reason to depart far from our own types; though I confess, even here, to a tendency to eclecticism of a chastened kind, and to a desire for liberty to unite in some degree the merits of the different styles.' Many but certainly not all of Scott's churches were repetitive and they could be, frankly, a little dull. Nevertheless, because of his enthusiasms, his knowledge and the fecundity of his office, he was, as Michael Hall has written, 'a pivotal link between the generation of Pugin and that of the late Gothic revival.'[125] From the hundreds of churches designed by the Scott office, which became known as the 'Spring Gardens Academy,' the best as well as representative examples are illustrated here.

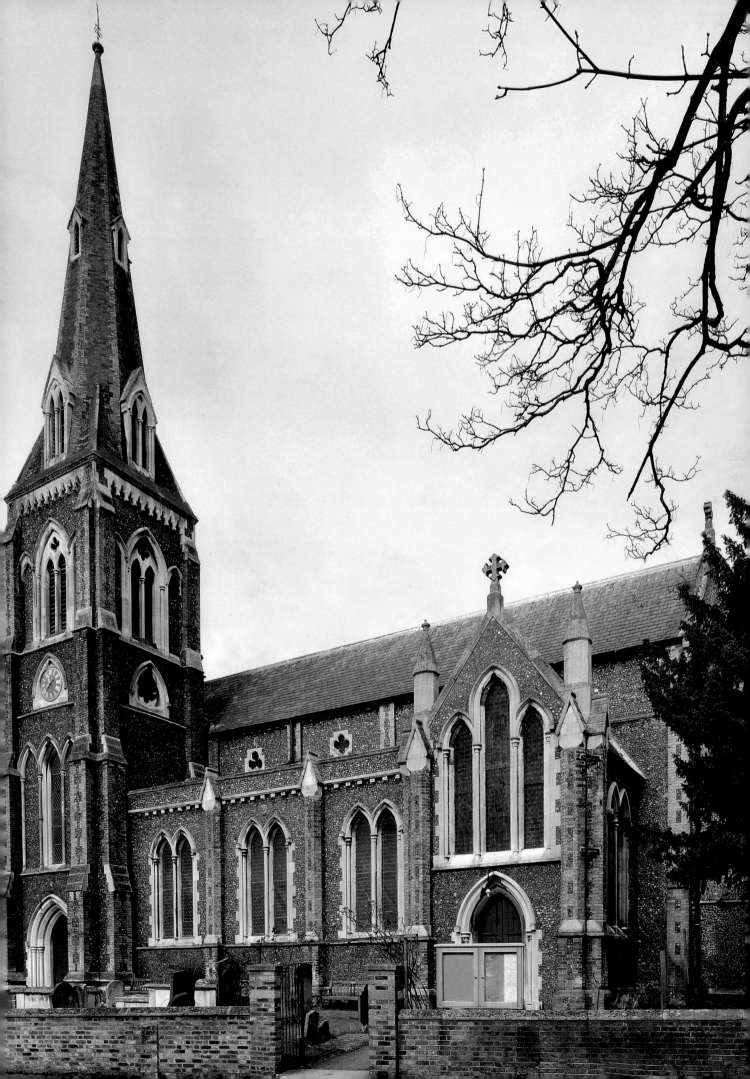

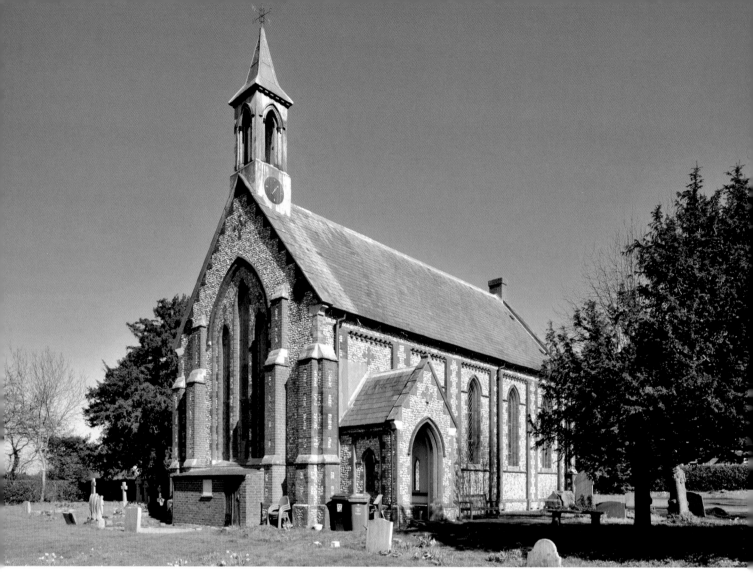

HANWELL, ST MARY 1841
PREVIOUS PAGE: St Mary's, Hanwell, Middlesex, built in 1841 and photographed by Geoff Brandwood in 2011; the best of Scott's early churches in the Early English style with lancet windows, having a fine steeple with a broach spire.

FLAUNDEN, HERTS, ST MARY MAGDALENE 1838
ABOVE: St Mary Magdalene, Flaunden, Hertfordshire, photographed by Geoff Brandwood in 2011: Scott's first church, designed for his uncle, the Revd Samuel King, in 1838, which he later dismissed as a 'poor barn', but remarkable for the early use of structural polychromy by combining flint and red brick.

LINCOLN, ST NICHOLAS 1839–40
RIGHT: St Nicholas, Lincoln, photographed in 2014: an early church, built 1839–40, and the first of seven with 'radical errors' which Scott soon came to regret.

CAMBERWELL, ST GILES' 1842–44

ABOVE: St Giles', Camberwell, as built in 1842–44 as depicted in an early lithograph. The old parish church had burned in 1841 and Scott & Moffatt had won the competition for a new church (see p. 31). This design was not built as Scott responded to the criticisms of the Cambridge Camden Society and to the example of Pugin and came up with an entirely new design: cruciform, 'Transitional' in style (i.e., combining Early English and Decorated) with a magnificent steeple over the crossing. Scott later recalled how his 'conversion to the exclusive use of real material came to its climax during the progress of this work' and the result was the best 'correct' Gothic church of its time, worthy of comparison with the work of his hero Pugin (also see frontispiece).

RIGHT: Scott's original five-bay gabled stone reredos survives today, with later colouring. Above is the east window, made by Ward & Nixon and designed by Edmund Oldfield, inspired by the thirteenth-century glass at Chartres on the advice of John Ruskin.

WORSLEY, LANCS, ST MARK'S 1844–46

LEFT: St Mark's Worsley, Lancashire, photographed by Geoff Brandwood in 2010. This grand church in Decorated Gothic on the outskirts of Manchester was built in 1844–46 at the expense of Lord Francis Egerton, later Earl of Ellesmere.

BELOW: The interior of the Worsley church, photographed in 1971 by Gordon Barnes, on an ecclesiologically correct plan with generous chancel, carved capitals and general sophistication in the handling of Decorated Gothic, shows how much Scott had learned in just a few years.

NIKOLAIKIRCHE, HAMBURG 1845–80

RIGHT: Scott had won the 1844 competition for rebuilding the Nikolaikirche in Hamburg after the 1842 fire with an accomplished essay in German Gothic: Germany, like England, then being full of enthusiasm for reviving the Medieval. Construction began in 1846 on a more elaborate design with transepts. This woodcut of the 1860s by A. Koch published in *L'Univers Illustré* shows the body of the church near completion with work beginning on the great west steeple.

LEFT: The Nikolaikirche was consecrated in 1863 but the colossal west tower and spire, 483 feet (147 metres) high, was not completed until 1874 when – for just two years – it was the tallest structure in the world.

RIGHT: Scott's great steeple, overlooking the Hopfenmarkt, was the highest as well as one of the finest things he ever achieved. This photograph was published in the *National Geographic Magazine* in 1933.

BELOW LEFT: The plan and an interior view of the chancel of the Nikolaikirche as published in *The Architect* in 1871. The last part of the church to be built was the baptistery to the south of the great steeple, completed in 1880.

BELOW FAR LEFT: The interior of the Nikolaikirche, shown here in the revised design with transepts published in *The Builder* in 1858, was very tall in relation to its width and so typical of Continental Gothic.

Swindon, St Mark's 1845–46

RIGHT: St Mark's, Swindon, Wiltshire, photographed in 2011, was built in 1845–46 to serve New Swindon adjacent to the locomotive works of the Great Western Railway. John Betjeman, who held it in affection, described it as one of 'those hard-looking buildings founded by Victorian piety'[126] but it is unusual in having its main entrance under a tower picturesquely sited at the west end of the north aisle.

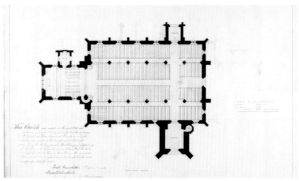

ABOVE: The plan for St Mark's, submitted to the Incorporated Church Building Society, shows an orthodox, ecclesiologically correct church, with a long, separate chancel and a nave with two aisles.

LEFT: The interior of St Mark's is typical of Scott's first mature churches, Decorated Gothic in style, with elegant arcades. The chancel was subsequently lengthened.

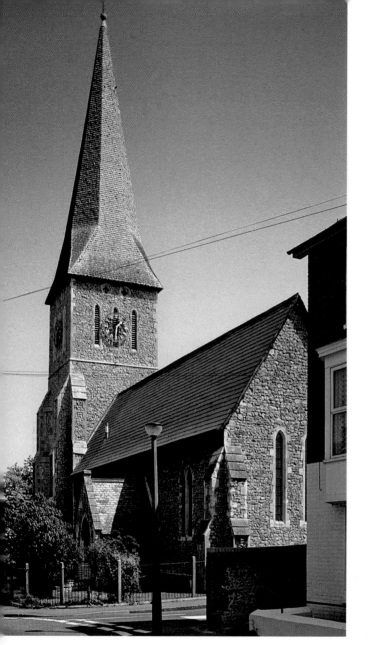

RAMSGATE, CHRIST CHURCH 1846–48

LEFT: Christ Church, Ramsgate, Kent, with its splay-foot spire, has a convincing rural Kentish character. It was built in 1846–48 as an Anglican riposte to the locally suspect Roman Catholic church of St Augustine being built next to his home by Pugin, to whose writings and buildings Scott owed to much. Photograph of 1998.

ISLINGTON, ST MATTHEW'S 1847–48

ABOVE RIGHT: St Matthew's, City Road, in Islington has gone. This photograph shows it in 1946 after bombing in the Second World War. It was built in 1847–48 in Kentish ragstone, that material much used for churches at the time although it weathered so unattractively. Set back from a main road, St Mark's did not have the character of a 'town church'. In his *London Churches: Ancient & Modern*, T. Francis Bumpus noted that the 'graceful steeple' was modelled on that of Long Sutton in Lincolnshire.

RIGHT: The interior of St Mary's in 1946 after bombing and before demolition. Bumpus wrote that the interior was 'solemn and devotional and exhibits careful stone carving and stained glass, some of the latter being exceedingly good'.

LEEDS, HOLBECK, ST JOHN THE EVANGELIST 1847–50

ABOVE: The Church of St John the Evangelist at Holbeck in Leeds, built in 1847–50, disappeared shortly before the Second World War; the only record of its appearance is this watercolour interior perspective which was exhibited at the Royal Academy in 1851. The vaulted church was modelled on the Temple Church in London. When that was bombed, H. S. Goodhart-Rendel recalled in 1958, 'I found it consoling to reflect that Sir Gilbert Scott's miniature copy of it in the slums of Leeds would display the beauty of its form to future generations. When, the other day, I hunted for it, map in hand, it was gone … If the choir of the Temple Church had not risen again, the copy, although having had little value while the original was standing, would have become a treasure of the second order.'[127]

WESTMINSTER, ST MATTHEW'S 1849–51

ABOVE: Only the first four storeys of the steeple of St Matthew's, Westminster, shown in this lithograph of 1850, were ever built. The body of the church was built in 1849–51 in what was then a notorious slum.

RIGHT: The interior of St Matthew's, Westminster, photographed by Gordon Barnes in 1967. Because of the awkward shape of the site, Scott gave the church a separate tower to the south to act as an entrance as well as an additional south aisle. This was separated from the main south aisle by an unusual arcade with segmental arches. This photograph shows the interior before the fire of 1977 which destroyed the furnishings, including the screen by Scott's former pupil, G. F. Bodley (who had worked on the original design). St Matthew's was subsequently reconstructed by Donald Buttress.

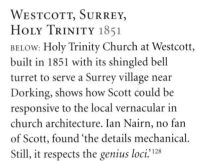

SWINDON, CHRIST CHURCH 1850–51

LEFT: Christ Church, Scott's second church in Swindon, was built in 1850–51 high up in the Old Town to replace an earlier church. This photograph, taken in 2014, shows the commanding west tower and spire.

WESTCOTT, SURREY, HOLY TRINITY 1851

BELOW: Holy Trinity Church at Westcott, built in 1851 with its shingled bell turret to serve a Surrey village near Dorking, shows how Scott could be responsive to the local vernacular in church architecture. Ian Nairn, no fan of Scott, found 'the details mechanical. Still, it respects the *genius loci*.'[128]

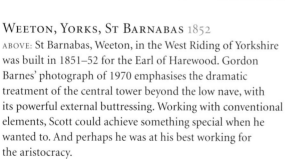

Weeton, Yorks, St Barnabas 1852

ABOVE: St Barnabas, Weeton, in the West Riding of Yorkshire was built in 1851–52 for the Earl of Harewood. Gordon Barnes' photograph of 1970 emphasises the dramatic treatment of the central tower beyond the low nave, with its powerful external buttressing. Working with conventional elements, Scott could achieve something special when he wanted to. And perhaps he was at his best working for the aristocracy.

ABOVE TOP: The porch of St Barnabas is remarkable for its use of cusping, a feature conventionally found in window tracery or open arcades.

ABOVE BELOW: Barnes' 1970 photograph is looking west from the chancel to the aisles nave beyond the space under the tower.

Rugby, Holy Trinity 1852–53

ABOVE: Holy Trinity Church was a fine work in Geometrical
Decorated in the centre of Rugby, built in 1852–53. This
photograph was taken in 1978, four years after it was declared
redundant. Despite the Secretary of State recommending, after
a non-statutory public inquiry, that this Grade A-listed church
should not be demolished, despite years of neglect, it was pulled
down by the Diocese of Coventry in 1981.

DONCASTER, ST GEORGE'S 1853–58

RIGHT: The old parish church of Doncaster in the West Riding of Yorkshire was destroyed by fire in 1853 and Scott was chosen to rebuild it. This contemporary lithograph by F. Bedford was taken from one of the perspective drawings commissioned by Scott of his design for the new church. It should be compared with the original church, illustrated on page 39.

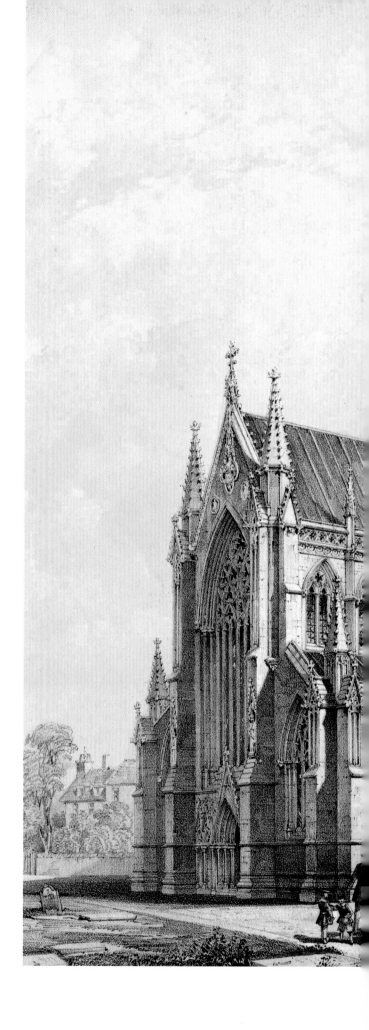

ABOVE: Doncaster Parish Church seen from the south-west in a photograph of the 1860s. Scott reproduced the general lines of the old church with its conspicuously high central crossing tower, but translated its Perpendicular Gothic style into his favourite Geometrical Decorated (and later regretted not reproducing the original tower). Nikolaus Pevsner wrote that this was 'the proudest and most cathedral-like of this fabulously busy and successful architect's parish churches'. [129]

RIGHT: The interior of St George's soon after completion, showing the elaborate carving of the capitals and the original reredos, pulpit and reading desk – all extant today. In the design of some of these features Scott had to endure the interference of his 'tormentor': the local grandee and bully, E. B. Denison, later Lord Grimthorpe.

RIGHT: The interior of the new St George's Doncaster as it looked at the time of its consecration in 1858 as depicted in the *Illustrated London News*. The new church is larger than the old as more accommodation was needed.

Dresden, Longton, Stoke, Church of the Resurrection 1853

LEFT: The Church of the Resurrection at Dresden, Longton, in the Staffordshire Potteries dates from 1853, i.e., contemporary with Scott's rebuilding of Doncaster Church, so may well seem the 'architectural mystery' that Pevsner found it. The use of red and glazed purple bricks reflects the incipient vogue for structural polychromy, while the polygonal apse, with its gables, is clearly of Continental inspiration. Whether this small but strikingly unusual church was by Scott or by a talented assistant in the office must be a matter for speculation. Photograph of 2011 by Geoff Brandwood.

RIGHT: The interior of the Church of the Resurrection at Dresden, photographed by Geoff Brandwood in 2011, is as remarkable as the exterior: arcades of red and yellow brick rise from simple brick piers in a manner which might seem to anticipate the later work of Butterfield. This church originally had but one aisle; a south aisle was added in 1873 by another hand.

ST. PAUL'S EPISCOPAL CHURCH, DUNDEE.

DUNDEE, ST PAUL'S EPISCOPAL 1853–55

ABOVE: St Paul's Episcopal; Church was commissioned by Alexander Penrose Forbes, Bishop of Brechin and Rector of Dundee, who was strongly influenced by the ideals of the Oxford Movement. The church was built in 1853–55. The site was hemmed in but the church was given prominence by the steeple – once the highest in Scotland and seen here in a woodcut published in the *Civil Engineer & Architect's Journal* – placed on an eminence at the top of a flight of steps where Dundee's castle once stood. Scott was clearly concerned to give this a Scottish character, and the tower was modelled on the Medieval tower of Dundee Parish Church.

ABOVE: The interior of St Paul's, Dundee, seen here in a photograph of 2013 by Geoff Brandwood, is tall and spacious. The nave arcade piers are very tall and very slender; there is no clerestory and light comes in from the large aisle windows placed under transverse gabled bays. The reredos, by Scott, was installed in 1870 in the stone-vaulted apsidal chancel. St Paul's was elevated to cathedral status in 1905.

TREFNANT, DENBIGHSHIRE, CLWYD, HOLY TRINITY 1855

ABOVE: Holy Trinity Church at Trefnant in Denbighshire, built 1853–55 as a memorial to Colonel and Mrs Salusbury of Galltfaenen Hall by their two daughters, shows that, on occasion, Scott could play with High Victorian 'mannerism' as the best of them. This small but expensive church in a Welsh village, photographed in 2013 by Geoff Brandwood, is powerfully massed, with the composition given added drama by the strong buttresses.

LEFT: The treatment of this door and canopy at Trefnant is not conventionally derived from Medieval precedent but a powerful and original composition in Gothic terms.

RIGHT: The interior at Trefnant has marble columns, a splendid marble font and magnificent carving, but the general effect today, recorded in this photograph by Geoff Brandwood, is now spoiled by the barbarous removal of the plaster from the east wall and from the tympanum above the chancel arch with its unusual secondary relieving arch.

LEFT: The fine capitals at Trefnant were carved by J. Blinstone, a local man who had been encouraged by Scott to study French carving at the Architectural Museum and who then, in a Ruskinian manner, studied natural specimens. The results surely justified his trip to London.

HALEY HILL, HALIFAX, ALL SOULS 1856–59

RIGHT: All Souls', Haley Hill, built by the worsted manufacturer, Edward Akroyd, M.P., in 1855–59 on a high, sloping site overlooking Halifax to serve his workforce in the nearby new suburb of Akroyden, was – as far as Scott was concerned – 'on the whole, my best church.' This woodcut, published in *The Builder* in 1859, the year the church was consecrated, shows the asymmetrically placed west steeple and the elevated site. The style used was Scott's favourite: English Decorated of the late thirteenth century, when 'the style attained its highest perfection' according to *The Ecclesiologist*.

BELOW: This interior perspective by J. Drayton Wyatt, published in *The Ecclesiologist* in 1860, shows the painting above the chancel arch of *The Adoration of the Lamb* which has since disappeared. This church was more English than French in style, with a square-ended chancel.

STOKE NEWINGTON, ST MARY'S 1965

ABOVE: The new church of St Mary in Stoke Newington (the old church still stands nearby) was one of Scott's largest in London. Here, as at Dundee, there is no clerestory and aisles are lit from tall windows below gabled roofs at right-angles to the body of the church – a feature which has English precedent but is German in origin. Otherwise this was one of Scott's most French designs, with its apsidal chancel, round columns and simple Geometrical window tracery. Francis Bumpus thought that the 'view of St Mary's from the north-east presents one of the finest pieces of architectural grouping in the Metropolis,' but the tremendous west steeple, inspired by examples in Normandy, was largely the work of John Oldrid Scott and was only completed in 1890. Photograph by Gordon Barnes, 1965.

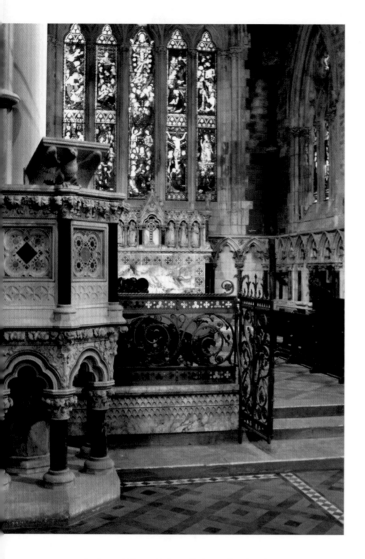

ABOVE: A view of the pulpit and chancel taken in 2008. The materials and the workmanship was of the very best: the superb metalwork was by Francis Skidmore of Coventry; the stained glass by Hardman.

LEFT: The interior of All Souls as it looked in 1968, photographed by Gordon Barnes, showing the fine carving and figure sculpture – much of it by J. B. Philip.

SHIRLEY, SURREY, ST JOHN THE EVANGELIST 1856
ABOVE: The Church of St John the Evangelist in the (then) village of Shirley near Croydon in Surrey, built 1855–56, is full of understated felicities and has an appropriate countrified air. The west tower with its low splay-foot spire, was originally intended to be taller. Ruskin's parents are buried in the churchyard. Photograph of 2010.

WOOLWICH DOCKYARD CHAPEL 1859

BELOW: The Woolwich Dockyard Chapel, built in 1857–59, is shown here in a print after a drawing by J. D. Wyatt. It had Scott's favourite transverse-gabled aisle, polychromatic brickwork, a Continental-looking apse and a fancy staircase-turret. After it became redundant in 1923, the whole was rebuilt further south in 1932–33 on Rochester Way to serve, as St Barnabas Church, the new Well Hall Estate, but in a rather smaller and simplified form.

RIGHT: Ignoring the theories and prejudices of Pugin and Ruskin, Scott was happy to employ thin iron columns to support both the roof and the galleries in this military chapel designed for a large congregation. When the building was re-erected in Eltham it was not so tall and only the upper parts of the iron columns were reused as the galleries were omitted. This church was gutted in 1944 and these columns disappeared in the post-war rebuilding.

❧ Gothic for the Steam Age

Ranmore Common, Dorking, Surrey, St Barnabas 1859

LEFT: St Barnabas at Ranmore Common near Dorking in Surrey was built 1857–59 to serve those who worked on the Denbies Estate. It is a grand estate church and is one of Scott's happiest ecclesiastical creations. The builder was George Cubitt, M.P., later Baron Ashcombe, whose father, the celebrated builder Thomas Cubitt, had built Denbies nearby. This is not one of Scott's formulaic churches: the splendid crossing tower is octagonal and every detail was carefully considered. Cubitt's country house was demolished in the 1950s, leaving Scott's church almost in splendid isolation; the estate is now a vineyard. Photographs taken in 2011.

RIGHT: This photograph shows part of the south transept and shows the quality of the Bath stone, combined with a facing of flint cobbles, of which the church is constructed as well as the unusual form of the small door.

BELOW: The surprise of the interior is the ribbed vault over the crossing, where Scott used squinch arches to support the octagon over the square space, the whole treated in an elaborate and sculptural manner, enhanced with fine carving.

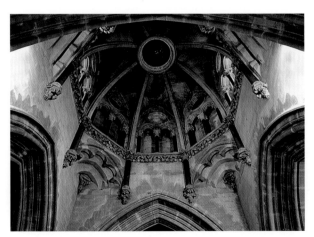

HAWKHURST, HIGHGATE, KENT, ALL SAINTS 1859–61

ABOVE: All Saints at Hawkhurst in Kent, seen here in an old postcard, has nave and two aisles under separate roofs so no clerestory and a steeple unusually placed at the east end of the south aisle. It was built in 1859–61 at the expense of the incumbent, the Revd H. A. Jeffreys. *The Ecclesiologist* thought it 'a careful rendering of rural Church architecture of South England' and for David Cole it is 'the best small church of the middle period' of Scott's career.

SHERBORNE, ALL SAINTS 1862–64

LEFT: All Saints, Sherborne, in Warwickshire is a particularly splendid, and expensive, estate church by Scott, photographed here in 2012. An older village church was rebuilt in 1862–64 by Louisa Anne Ryland, the daughter of Samuel Ryland, wire-manufacturer of Birmingham, who had bought the estate in 1837. The plan of the church is conventional, but the steeple – French in inspiration – particularly magnificent. David Cole thought this Scott's 'best large church, though it is not at all influenced by local forms.'

BELOW: The interior of All Saints is sumptuous, thanks to excellent carving of the capitals by William Brindley of Farmer & Brindley and the introduction of colour by using marble shafts on the nave piers: pink Ipplepen and green verde antico. Thomas Garner, Scott's pupil and the future partner of G. F. Bodley, acted as clerk of works on this commission.

SHACKLEFORD, SURREY, ST MARY'S 1865

RIGHT: St Mary's, Shackleford, is a rather grand church for a Surrey village, photographed here in 2011. It was built in 1865 of the local Burgate stone and has tall crossing tower, countrified with a short splay-foot spire. It is perhaps surprising that in the mid-1860s Scott was still giving some of his churches an apse rather than a square English east end.

DERBY, ST ANDREW'S 1864–81

LEFT: St Andrew's, Derby, has gone, demolished in 1971. The photograph here was taken by G. B. Mason for the National Buildings Record in 1942. The body of this austere church was built in 1864–66. In 1872, Scott's younger brother, the Revd Melville Horne Scott, became vicar and he determined that the fine north-west tower with its broach spire was completed in 1880–81.

134 ❦ GOTHIC FOR THE STEAM AGE

KENSINGTON, ST MARY ABBOTS 1872

RIGHT: St Mary Abbots, built 1869-72 on a prominent site in Kensington to replace a decrepit seventeenth century building, must be Scott's best known church in London. This is unfortunate as, although expensive and well appointed, St Mary Abbots, built of ragstone, is rather conventional, and a little dull. Scott was appointed in 1868 as his 'European reputation renders it altogether unnecessary on the part of the Committee to enter on any justification of their choice'.[130] This photograph shows the new church in c.1872 before the tall steeple was built.

LEFT: The interior of St Mary Abbots, photographed in 2014. Although some fine furnishings and stained glass survived bombing in the Second World War, the interior might seem to confirm Francis Bumpus' opinion that, 'through the whole of St Mary's we perceive that spirit of academism, that fearfulness of overstepping the limits of conventionalism, from which the architect could never free himself'.

OVERLEAF: Scott's design for St Mary Abbots, as published in the *Building News* in 1881 – the year the steeple was completed. Oddly, although this church was designed in Scott's favourite Transitional style for the West End of London, its inspiration was partly Scottish. The nave was modelled on that of Paisley Abbey and the west front, with its triple tall windows, is strongly reminiscent of that of Dunblane Cathedral. An impressive and unusual feature are the double-gabled transepts.

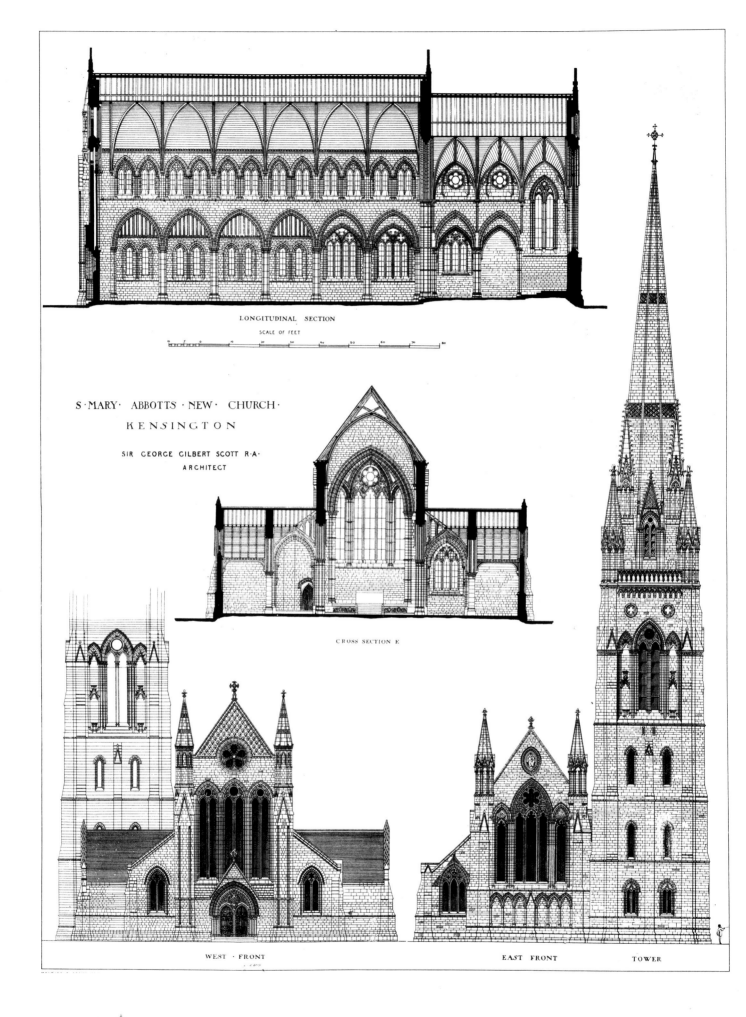

LONGITUDINAL SECTION

SCALE OF FEET

S·MARY· ABBOTTS ·NEW· CHURCH·

KENSINGTON

SIR GEORGE GILBERT SCOTT R·A·
ARCHITECT

CROSS SECTION E

WEST · FRONT

EAST FRONT

TOWER

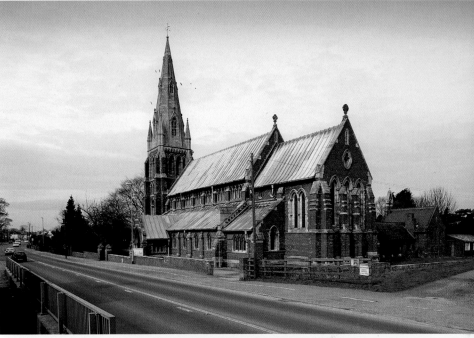

FULNEY, SPALDING, LINCOLN, ST PAUL'S 1877–80

ABOVE: One of the contract drawings, dated 1877, for building St Paul's Church in Fulney outside Spalding, Lincolnshire. The church was built in 1877–80 and paid for by Miss Charrington of Spalding.

ABOVE RIGHT: St Paul's, Fulney, was one of Scott's last churches, and it is not possible to know whether he had much to do with the design or whether it was entirely delegated to John Oldrid Scott or another assistant in the office. Photograph by English Heritage 2007.

RIGHT: This church has many elements typical of Scott's work over the preceding four decades, but there are some distinctive features – notably the alternating round and clustered columns and, above all, the round blank arches uniting pairs of bays of the nave arcades.

CATHEDRALS

Scott also had the opportunity to design large churches of cathedral status, but these were all outside England as no new Anglican cathedrals were commissioned at home during his lifetime (the new diocese of Truro was only created in 1877). These cathedrals were mostly in far-flung parts of the British Empire: Newfoundland, South Africa and New Zealand. Scott was deeply interested in colonial ecclesiastical architecture. As Alex Bremner has observed, 'Scott may have been notorious for delegating and entrusting considerable amounts of work to his assistants, but when the opportunity arose to design a cathedral, he seems to have entered upon the enterprise enthusiastically, opening up a correspondence with his clients that discloses a keen level of commitment and oversight.'[131] The problem with such buildings was that it was difficult to control the building process at a distance (Scott never travelled beyond Europe) and that, with limited funds available, they were often no larger than many parish churches in England, therefore, as Scott claimed for his cathedral design for Edinburgh, 'the church must, both within and without, bear such unmistakable credentials of high dignity as to be obviously suited to its rank as the chief church of the diocese …' This Episcopalian cathedral in Scotland was one of Scott's last and noblest works, won in competition in 1873 and not completed until after his death.

EDINBURGH, ST MARY'S

RIGHT: St Mary's Episcopal Cathedral was Scott's only cathedral in the British Isles. Designs were invited in 1872 from three English and three Scottish architects after the Walker sisters, heirs to Sir Patrick Walker, the developer of Easter Coates, left money for the building of a cathedral at the end of Melville Place. Scott submitted two designs; the assessor, Ewan Christian, favoured the entry by G. E. Street but the newly arrived Bishop Cotterill supported Scott and work began in 1874. This photograph by George Washington Wilson shows the cathedral soon after building was consecrated in 1879 but before the intended west towers were built under the direction of Scott's grandson, Charles Marriott Oldrid Scott in 1913–17. Today, St Mary's has three stone spires, like Lichfield Cathedral in England.

NEWFOUNDLAND, ST JOHN'S

ABOVE: Following a fire which in 1846 destroyed the town of St John's in Newfoundland, Scott was appointed the following year to design a new Anglican cathedral. Because of the need for economy together with the hostile climate, Scott sent out an austere design in the Early English style, but this was a fine cruciform composition, worthy of the sloping site, with a central crossing tower, shown here in a fine perspective drawing reproduced as a woodcut in the *Illustrated London News* in 1849. The history of the project was unfortunate: the nave only was consecrated in 1850; the transepts and choir were built in the 1880s under the distant direction of G. G. Scott junior, but in 1892 another fire in St John's damaged the cathedral and it was not restored and finished until 1905.

EDINBURGH, ST MARY'S

RIGHT: The interior of St Mary's Cathedral looking east, photographed by George Washington Wilson. The architecture is grand and austere; Scott wrote in his report that he had been 'most impressed by the earlier phase of the First Pointed period which especially unites the architecture of Scotland with that of Northern England and is one capable, I think, of the greatest amount of simplicity and any amount of beauty'.

New Zealand, Christ Church

RIGHT: Scott was first approached to design a cathedral for the settlement of Canterbury in New Zealand in 1858. A hybrid design was sent out in 1862 for a building with a timber structure within stone walls, but Bishop Harper and others opted for a building entirely of local stone. Work began on this very English-looking building in 1864 and was completed in 1881 under the direction of Benjamin Mountfort, who made slight changes to the design of the semi-detached steeple. This collapsed in the 2011 earthquakes and the rest is threatened with demolition.

ST. MARYS CATH. EDINBURGH. LOOKING EAST. 2580. G.W.W.

MONUMENTS & MEMORIALS

Thanks to a culture of mourning which has been called 'the Victorian Celebration of Death', it is not surprising that memorials, monuments and gravestones formed a significant part of Scott's output – working with sculptors he designed over sixty of them, several exported to India – and he was responsible for the most famous and prominent public memorial of his time, one that now seems so well to express the ideals of the mid-Victorian age: the Albert Memorial in Kensington. Scott's design developed the model of the Gothic canopy or cross, an idea already adopted in Britain and elsewhere by other architects for public monuments. This Medieval form was used by Scott for public memorials both at the very beginning of his career and near the end, in Oxford and Wisbech respectively. He also developed a different and novel form for memorials which was a Gothic version of the Classical monumental column inspired by Italian Gothic precedents. This, consisting of a cylindrical shaft of granite supporting a four-sided sculptural tabernacle, first rose behind the tomb of Sir Charles Hotham in Melbourne, Australia, and was described as a 'somewhat novel and exquisite piece of work' and by *The Ecclesiologist* as a 'bold and beautiful experiment'. Soon after, the idea was developed for Westminster School's memorial to the Crimean War and Scott used it again for the memorial in the village of Ford in Northumberland commissioned by Louisa, Lady Waterford. As for tombs, the finest and certainly the most poignant are the two he designed for members of his own family – his wife and one of his sons – for two different Surrey churchyards, Tandridge and Petersham.

OXFORD, MARTYRS' MEMORIAL

RIGHT: The Martyrs' Memorial in Oxford was Scott's first essay in scholarly Gothic. In 1840 he was invited to enter a competition to design a memorial to commemorate the Protestant martyrs Cranmer, Latimer and Ridley who had been burned close to the site. The project was designed to counter the growing influence of 'Romanism' inspired by the Oxford Movement launched in 1833 within the Church of England (Pugin attacked its promoters as 'foul revilers, tyrants, usurpers, extortioners and liars'[132]). Scott's design, shown here in a perspective by Louis Haghe published as a lithograph in 1840 and based on the Eleanor Crosses and on Waltham Cross in particular, was chosen and carried out in 1841–43. At the same time he added a new north aisle to the nearby Medieval Church of St Mary Magdalen, which can be seen in the distance.

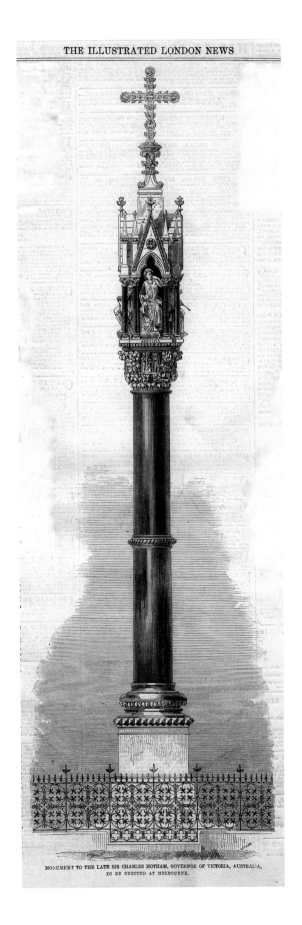

MONUMENT TO THE LATE SIR CHARLES HOTHAM, GOVERNOR OF VICTORIA, AUSTRALIA,
TO BE ERECTED AT MELBOURNE.

MELBOURNE, VICTORIA, SIR CHARLES HOTHAM

LEFT: Following the death of Sir Charles Hotham, the Governor of Victoria, in 1855, Lady Hotham travelled back from Australia to find a design for the tomb-monument to go over her husband's grave in Melbourne. She chose Scott, who came up with the novel idea of a tall cylindrical column surmounted by a four-sided Gothic tabernacle, illustrated here by a woodcut published in the *Illustrated London News* in 1858. Work began on the carving in the studio of the sculptor John Birnie Philip in 1857 and it was shipped out and installed in Melbourne the following year. Red granite was used for the column and tomb, Portland stone for the tabernacle.

WESTMINSTER SCHOOL, CRIMEAN WAR MONUMENT

RIGHT: Scott was clearly pleased with his design for a non-Classical monument for the Hotham tomb for he developed the idea for the 'Westminster Column', a memorial to the scholars of Westminster School killed in the recent war against Russia in the Crimea. This photograph of c.1861 taken from an upper floor of Scott's own Dean's Yard, however, shows the memorial soon after it was raised in Broad Sanctuary in 1858.

BELOW: The four-sided tabernacle on top of the column contains the seated figures of monarchs – Edward the Confessor, Henry III and Queens Elizabeth and Victoria – and is surmounted by St George and the dragon, all carved by Birnie Philip.

CALCUTTA, LADY CANNING

RIGHT: A third version of the Gothic column was raised in the village of Ford, Northumberland, for Louisa, Lady Waterford, whose sister, Charlotte Canning, the wife of Lord Canning, Viceroy of India, had died in Calcutta in 1861. Scott was asked to design her tomb, and came up with something different: a large flat tomb with an elaborate Gothic headstone cross, carved again by Birnie Philip. Made of white marble, it was shipped out to India in 1865 and placed over Lady Canning's grave in the grounds of at Barrackpore, the Viceroy's summer residence on the river Hooghly. As it soon deteriorated in the open air, the tomb was replaced by a replica and the original moved first, in 1873, to St Paul's Cathedral in Calcutta (where there is another monument by Scott and Philip to another Viceroy, Lord Elgin) and then to the north portico of St John's Church in Calcutta, where this photograph was taken in 2013.

KENSINGTON, PRINCE CONSORT NATIONAL MEMORIAL

BELOW: This watercolour perspective drawing shows Scott's winning design for the competition for the Prince Consort National Memorial held in 1862; the artist is not recorded. Scott presented this picture to Queen Victoria the following year. The drawing shows the Memorial as it was constructed in 1864–72 except that, in response to criticism, Scott heightened the spire; he later regretted this, writing that 'the greatest fault in the design … is that the flèche is too high'.

OPPOSITE: This photograph of the Albert Memorial was taken shortly after the gilded bronze figure of Prince Albert, by John Foley, was installed under the canopy in 1876.

PUBLIC BUILDINGS

Scott may have been primarily a church architect but his driving ambition made it certain that he would undertake a large public work if the opportunity arose; indeed, it has been suggested that he hoped he might be regarded as the principal State Architect. Like his hero Pugin, Scott was anxious to demonstrate that Gothic was not just a style suitable for churches but could be used successfully for all manner of building types. This was the argument developed in his influential book, *Remarks on Secular & Domestic Architecture, Present & Future*, first published in 1857. Scott insisted that Gothic was capable of 'development', that it was flexible and practical, that it could encompass new building technologies, like iron construction and plate glass, and was also not bound by the use of the pointed arch. The opportunity to test these theories in a public building came with the competition for new government offices in Whitehall. This farcical affair ended with Scott being obliged by the Prime Minister, Lord Palmerston, to design a Classical building. Nevertheless, the result is a distinguished work, an adornment to Whitehall and St James's Park, in which Scott showed himself adept as a planner and constructor, able to create grand and decorative formal spaces. Nor was his skill at secular Gothic wasted, for he was able to demonstrate the practicality of his approach in the new town hall at Preston and, with Scottish overtones, at the Albert Institute in Dundee while he continued to enter competitions for major public buildings in London (the Law Courts) and in Germany. Commissions for new hospitals also came Scott's way, with the Infirmary at Leeds and, on a smaller and more domestic scale, at Savernake in Wiltshire.

RIGHT: WHITEHALL, FOREIGN OFFICE
The most magnificent of Scott's interiors was the Banqueting Hall, shown here in a photograph by Adam Woolfit taken in 1992 following its rediscovery under partitions and inserted floors and its subsequent restoration.

BELOW: A view of the canopy above the figure of Albert; the mosaic in the pediment represents 'Poetry' and was by John Clayton of Clayton & Bell.

QUEEN · VICTORIA · AND · HER · PEOPLE

RIGHT: The Albert Memorial was not pure architecture and not purely Gothic in style. It was the creation of many artists and craftsmen and relied on symbolic sculpture, in both bronze and Portland stone, and on colour achieved by a variety of materials: stone, granite, marble, bronze, iron, mosaic, glass and gold. In this view, taken in 2010, the magnificent iron railings, by Francis Skidmore, can be seen along with the podium frieze behind with figures by Birnie Philip and Armstead. In the foreground is one of the four Continents placed at the outer corners: 'America' by John Bell. In the distance is the Royal Albert Hall, an associated structure that Scott had hoped to design as well, but in vain – thanks to Henry Cole.

WISBECH, CLARKSON MEMORIAL

ABOVE: The Clarkson Memorial in Wisbech, Cambridgeshire, is a posthumous work by Scott, seen here in a postcard of c.1956, in which he returned to the precedent of the Gothic Cross for inspiration. In response to a public campaign to erect a memorial to Thomas Clarkson, the great anti-slavery campaigner, a native of Wisbech, Scott produced a design in 1875 but it was not until 1880 that sufficient funds had been secured and the work was supervised by John Oldrid Scott. The figure of Clarkson under the canopy was by Farmer & Brindley. It may or may not be significant that by this time Scott's brother John had become vicar of Wisbech.

PETERSHAM CHURCHYARD, TOMB OF ALBERT HENRY SCOTT

ABOVE: Scott placed this tomb monument, of pink and grey granite embellished with red marble, over the grave in Petersham churchyard in Surrey in which his third son, Albert Henry Scott, was buried in 1865 when the family was living at the Manor House at Ham. Photograph of 2011.

TANDRIDGE CHURCHYARD, TOMB OF CAROLINE OLDRID SCOTT

BELOW: Scott's wife, Caroline Oldrid, died in 1872 when living at Rook's Nest near Godstone in Surrey and was buried nearby in Tandridge churchyard. Scott wrote that, 'I have designed what I trust will be a beautiful monument to my ever dearest Carry – it is to be a low altar tomb, parts of white marble and in part of polished granite. The upper stone which is of marble will have a very richly floriated cross, the foliage being partly conventionalised and partly natural, the latter carrying out her intense love of flowers and of botany. On either side of the cross two of the beatitudes will be inscribed … Round the dado will be medallions also symbolising her special virtues by emblematic figures …' Which of Scott's favourite artists and craftsmen carried out this work is not recorded.

PUBLIC BUILDINGS

Scott may have been primarily a church architect but his driving ambition made it certain that he would undertake a large public work if the opportunity arose; indeed, it has been suggested that he hoped he might be regarded as the principal State Architect. Like his hero Pugin, Scott was anxious to demonstrate that Gothic was not just a style suitable for churches but could be used successfully for all manner of building types. This was the argument developed in his influential book, *Remarks on Secular & Domestic Architecture, Present & Future*, first published in 1857. Scott insisted that Gothic was capable of 'development', that it was flexible and practical, that it could encompass new building technologies, like iron construction and plate glass, and was also not bound by the use of the pointed arch. The opportunity to test these theories in a public building came with the competition for new government offices in Whitehall. This farcical affair ended with Scott being obliged by the Prime Minister, Lord Palmerston, to design a Classical building. Nevertheless, the result is a distinguished work, an adornment to Whitehall and St James's Park, in which Scott showed himself adept as a planner and constructor, able to create grand and decorative formal spaces. Nor was his skill at secular Gothic wasted, for he was able to demonstrate the practicality of his approach in the new town hall at Preston and, with Scottish overtones, at the Albert Institute in Dundee while he continued to enter competitions for major public buildings in London (the Law Courts) and in Germany. Commissions for new hospitals also came Scott's way, with the Infirmary at Leeds and, on a smaller and more domestic scale, at Savernake in Wiltshire.

RIGHT: WHITEHALL, FOREIGN OFFICE
The most magnificent of Scott's interiors was the Banqueting Hall, shown here in a photograph by Adam Woolfit taken in 1992 following its rediscovery under partitions and inserted floors and its subsequent restoration.

WHITEHALL, GOVERNMENT OFFICES (FOREIGN OFFICE)

ABOVE: After much controversy, Scott's final design for the new Government Offices in the Classical manner insisted on by the prime minister, Lord Palmerston, was approved by Parliament in 1861. The St James's Park front of the combined Foreign and India Offices is picturesquely asymmetrical with a belvedere tower, an arrangement which Scott acknowledged was based on a sketch by Matthew Digby Wyatt. Scott may have fought hard for Gothic, but his Classical building is nevertheless a distinguished and sophisticated design of some originality.

LEFT: The whole block comprising the Foreign and India Offices at the St James's Park end of the site and the Home and Colonial Offices facing Whitehall contains one large quadrangle approached from an arched entrance in King Charles Street. This photograph, taken in 1975, shows its northern side.

ABOVE RIGHT: Scott was commissioned to design the new Home & Colonial Offices in 1868. This woodcut, published in the *Builder* in 1874, shows the central portion facing Parliament Street now shorn of the intended porte-cochère as well as the corner towers owing to the parsimony of Gladstone's Liberal government. The figurative carving in the spandrels and in the tympani of the arches, by H. H. Armstead, and the figures on the parapet, by J. B. Philip, were, however, carried out as Scott intended.

JUNE 20, 1874.]　THE BUILDER.　525

THE NEW COLONIAL OFFICE, PARLIAMENT STREET: CENTRAL PORTION.
SIR G. GILBERT SCOTT, R.A., ARCHITECT.

ABOVE: Scott's skill in handling decorative elements and his delight in using iron construction in an honest and straightforward manner are evident on the ceiling of the Foreign Secretary's room, where the beams are both structural and ornamental – and not at all Classical. Photograph by Adam Woolfit.

BELOW LEFT: Scott's finest interior in the Foreign Office is the Ambassadors' stair rising to the Foreign Secretary's room and the principal reception rooms, a grand conception intended to impress foreign diplomats and one which attest to Scott's skill and virtuosity. This photograph was taken in 1975.

BELOW: The original interiors of the Home & Colonial Offices were rather less grand and expensive. This photograph, taken in 1975 before restoration and modernization of the building commenced, shows the entrance hall of the Home Office.

PRESTON TOWN HALL

OPPOSITE: The clock tower in Fishergate, seen here in a photograph of c.1935, was the tallest in Britain after that of the Palace of Westminster. Preston Town Hall was gutted by fire in 1947; the roof was burned off and the clock tower very badly damaged. No attempt was made to restore the building – the town council by now had further accommodation nearby – and the ruins stood forlornly through the 1950s until, despite public protest, they were cleared away in 1962.

LEFT: Preston Town Hall was Scott's first important public building to be commissioned outside London, the Lancashire market town having developed in the first half of the nineteenth-century into an industrial centre. Built in 1862–66 on the site of the old Moot Hall, it was an opportunity for Scott to realise some of the ideas he had developed in his Gothic design for the Government Offices. This contemporary steel engraving shows the clock tower and principal front facing Fishergate, with open arcades on the ground floor.

ABOVE: Scott's Town Hall had fine interiors, to judge by surviving photographs taken in the 1930s. This one shows the upstairs lobby, lined with busts of local worthies.

LEWES FITZROY LIBRARY

LEFT: The Fitzroy Memorial Library in Lewes, East Sussex, is one of Scott's most intriguing secular Gothic buildings. It was built in 1862 by Hannah Mayer Rothschild in memory of her husband, Henry Fitzroy, M.P. for Lewes, and stands in the High Street on land purchased from the London, Brighton and South Coast Railway, whose line to Uckfield once ran almost next door. The public borrowing library was a large top-lit room with an octagonal timber galleried structure placed within the square. Given to the town in 1862 and closed as a library in 1955, the building was neglected and partially demolished in 1970 before being rescued by James Franks and his family in 1976, who restored it as a house. Fitzroy was made Commissioner of Public Works by Lord Palmerston during the Foreign Office controversy and Scott felt he was an ally. Photograph 2015.

WILTSHIRE, SAVERNAKE HOSPITAL

LEFT: The small 'cottage hospital' at Savernake near Marlborough, Wiltshire, was built in 1871–72 and in making its design Scott was clearly aware of the new 'Old English' style being used by Richard Norman Shaw and other younger architects. In the perspective of Scott's design published in *The Builder* the central projecting bay above the entrance and board room is shown as half-timbered, but as built this was tile-hung. The flanking polygonal bay windows lit the two principal wards, one for men and one for women. From an early postcard.

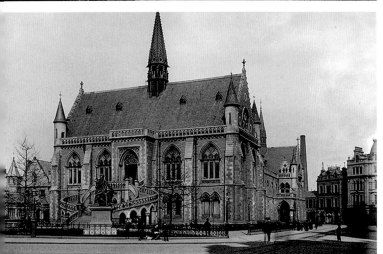

DUNDEE, ALBERT INSTITUTE

LEFT: The Albert Institute Co. Ltd was formed in Dundee to erect a building to house a free library, museum, picture gallery and public hall in memory of the Prince Consort. Scott was appointed architect in 1864 and the first phase, with a surprisingly curvaceous staircase – similar that that at Drumlanrig Castle – leading to the entrance to the first floor hall, was built in 1865–68. Scott used here for the first time a style which he claimed to have invented, a secular Gothic manner with Scottish features added. The building was extended in 1871 and in 1887 in Scott's style by David Mackenzie II and then by William Alexander and is now known as the McManus, Dundee's Art Gallery and Museum. This photograph was taken by the local photographer Alexander Wilson in the 1890s.

LEEDS GENERAL INFIRMARY

RIGHT: The Leeds General Infirmary was one of the first hospitals in Britain to use the pavilion plan of ward blocks pioneered at Lariboisière Hospital at Vincennes, Paris, built in 1846–54 and published in 1859 in *Notes on Hospitals* by Florence Nightingale, whom Scott consulted. Before preparing his design, Scott visited this Paris hospital with Dr Chadwick, the Infirmary's chief physician, on a Continental tour with his wife in 1863 during which he inspected other new hospitals. Drawn by Drayton Wyatt, this plan was published in *The Builder* in 1864.

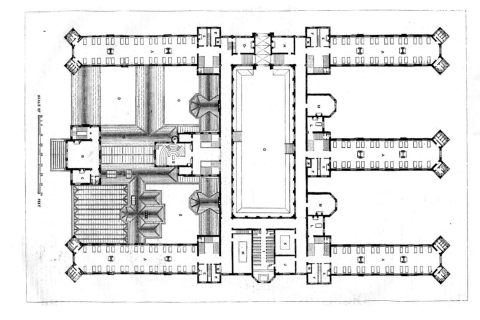

LEEDS GENERAL INFIRMARY

ABOVE: Leeds General Infirmary was built in 1863–69 to house 296 patients, replacing the eighteenth-century hospital by John Carr. Scott's appointment followed from his building Beckett's Bank in Leeds (page 175). The site was sloping and awkward. This photograph, taken in 2011, shows the principal entrance front in Great George Street. Built of red brick and sandstone, the hospital is similar in style to Scott's later hotel at St Pancras Station, but here Scott enjoyed exploiting the 45-degree geometry of the corner sanitary towers placed at the ends of the long ward pavilions.

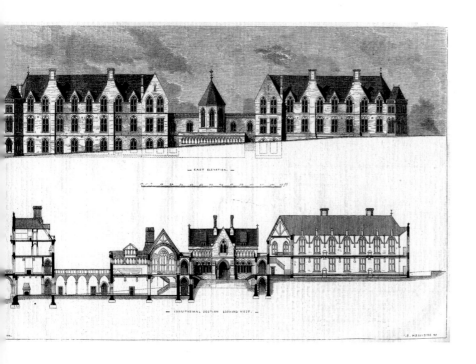

LEFT: This plate, drawn by Drayton Wyatt, showing the east or side elevation of the Leeds General Infirmary and a cross section from the entrance porte-cochère across the courtyard to the rear, northern front was also published in *The Builder* in 1864.

EDUCATIONAL

Scott's practice, like those of Butterfield, Alfred Waterhouse and his own former pupil, T. G. Jackson, benefited from the massive expansion of higher education in Britain in the mid-nineteenth century. The ancient universities in England – Oxford and Cambridge – reactionary Anglican institutions, were reformed during those decades to permit a wider and larger entry of undergraduates of all faiths and the teaching of a wider range of subjects. Scott was called on by several Oxbridge colleges to provide designs for new residential buildings, or a library, or a modern master's lodge, or a much larger new chapel or just to restore the old chapel and ancient buildings. In Cambridge (assisted by his son, G. G. Scott junior) he worked at St John's and King's Colleges and Peterhouse as well as for the University; at Oxford he was employed by six colleges in all, notably Exeter and New College. Elsewhere, in Scotland, the old college in Glasgow moved to an entirely new site and Scott was given the opportunity of designing the new buildings on Gilmorehill. He was even asked to send out designs to India for the new University of Bombay, although that commission ended unhappily. Scott also worked in several public schools which were, again, being reformed and expanded in the mid-Victorian years: Harrow, Rugby and Wellington. He was closely involved with one new public school in particular, Bradfield College, as he formed a friendship with its founder, the Revd Thomas Stevens, whose daughter, Mary Anne, would marry his second son, John Oldrid.

OXFORD, EXETER COLLEGE

RIGHT: Exeter College Chapel was the first in Oxford to have a stone vault, and in it Scott introduced a degree of polychromy. The success of the interior of the chapel partly relied on excellent craftsmanship: the stained glass was by Clayton & Bell; the mosaics by Antonio Salviati; the sculpture by John Birnie Philip assisted by John Lockwood Kipling; the gates of the screen separating the ante-chapel from the chapel were by Francis Skidmore. This photograph of 1870 by Henry Taunt shows the interior before canopies were placed over the stalls by G. F. Bodley. The historian E. A. Freeman thought the chapel 'the most glorious building in modern England'.[133]

BRIGHTON COLLEGE

ABOVE: Brighton College, the first public school in Sussex, was founded in 1845 by William Aldwin Soames to provide 'a thoroughly liberal and practical education in accordance with the principles of the established church'. The buildings were therefore Gothic. Won in competition, this was Scott's first important secular commission after the break up with Moffatt. He designed a three-sided court with a central entrance porch, all in flint and Caen stone; the central range was built in 1848–49. This photograph was taken in 2014; the Chapel on the left, added in 1858–59, was later greatly enlarged by Scott's former pupil T. G. Jackson.

LEFT: Scott continued to add buildings at Brighton College until Jackson took over in the 1880s. This early twentieth-century postcard shows the dormitory wing and headmaster's house added in 1852–53. This house presents an accomplished essay in asymmetry, almost High Victorian in character. The double height oriel supported on a buttress, a motif derived from Great Chalfield Manor (illustrated by the elder Pugin), would later be used by Street, Butterfield and Philip Webb.

ST. ANDREW'S CHURCH AND COLLEGE, BRADFIELD, BERKSHIRE.

BRADFIELD COLLEGE

ABOVE: Bradfield College in Berkshire was founded by the Revd Thomas Stevens, the local squarson, whom Scott had first met back in 1838 when he was a Poor Law Commissioner; he would become a close friend as well as a client. This 1865 woodcut published in the *Illustrated London News* shows, on the left, St Andrew's, the Medieval church of which Stevens was rector and which he and Scott extensively restored and enlarged in 1847–48, in places influenced by French rather than English precedents.

LEFT: This photograph by Geoff Brandwood, taken in 2011, shows the exterior of the flint and red brick Dining Hall, built in 1856, with its unusual triangular timber dormers. 'Of the buildings of the college,' Scott wrote, 'I do not claim to be the architect; it was not built out of hand, but grew of itself, bit by bit, as it was wanted, each part being planned by Mr Stevens, helped a little by myself or by my clerk, Mr Richard Coad. The hall is the part I may chiefly claim as my own.' Some later buildings were designed by Scott's second son, John Oldrid Scott, who was educated at the college (his elder brother had won a scholarship to Eton).

LEFT: The interior of the Dining Hall at Bradfield College is one of Scott's more remarkable creations, built like a country barn with an open timber roof supported by square piers of oak. It is also remarkable because the windows at the end of the hall were filled with stained glass made by Powells to a very early design by the young Edward Burne-Jones, made in 1857.

OXFORD, EXETER COLLEGE CHAPEL

ABOVE: The new chapel at Exeter College was Scott's first collegiate commission in Oxford, and one of his very finest creations, even if somewhat destructive in its advent. Scott was one of several architects who, in 1847, prepared designs to replace the college's 'debased' Jacobean chapel. Scott alone was commissioned in 1853 when the project was revived and when he was particularly enthusiastic for French thirteenth-century Gothic. As built in 1856–59, the replacement chapel was clearly inspired by the Sainte-Chapelle in Paris, which he knew well. This photograph, taken from a glass lantern slide, shows the chapel's dramatic height and the way it dominates the older buildings in the main quadrangle.

RIGHT: In his *History of the Gothic Revival*, published in 1872, Charles L. Eastlake illustrated the south porch of this 'stately building.' Both William Morris, Scott's future enemy and Edward Burne-Jones were undergraduates at Exeter College when his new Chapel was being proposed. The following decade, Scott's sent his third son, Albert, to study there.

OXFORD, EXETER COLLEGE LIBRARY

ABOVE: Scott was responsible for other new buildings at Exeter, including new Rector's Lodgings necessitated by the demolition of the old to build the chapel and a new range, with a gate tower, along Broad Street. He also designed on new Library on a site overlooking the Fellows' garden which had once been proposed for the new chapel. This detached building, begun in 1855 and seen here in an engraving published in 1858, is remarkable for its 'mural arcuation' on the first floor, with just a few small windows cut into a blank arcade, above which are notably handsome gabled dormers.

OXFORD, NEW COLLEGE

LEFT: At New College, Oxford, Scott restored the chapel. He also designed a range of stone-faced buildings along Holywell Street in 'collegiate Gothic' to cope with the college's expanding body of undergraduates. As designed, these were to be three storied but in 1872 the college insisted on adding an extra storey, making these buildings somewhat overbearing despite their bulk being broken by projecting bays, towers and gables.

CAMBRIDGE, ST JOHN'S COLLEGE, CHAPEL

ABOVE: Scott worked extensively in Cambridge. His largest commission came in 1862 from St John's College, where he enlarged the hall and built a new, detached Master's Lodge. His most conspicuous work, however, was the new Chapel, built in 1863–69. This was built to replace the college's small red-brick Tudor Gothic chapel (which, at one stage, Scott proposed retaining and enlarging). The new chapel, of stone, is similar in style and plan to Exeter College Chapel except that it is larger, with a larger ante-chapel and more English than French in character. It also has a conspicuous west tower, modelled on that of Pershore Abbey, which was to be paid for by a benefaction which never materialised, leaving the college somewhat embarrassed financially. This magnificent photograph, taken soon after completion, shows the new chapel from the east.

LEFT: The south side of the chapel with the site of the old chapel in the foreground: photograph taken in 2011.

LEFT: The interior of St John's College Chapel is similar in arrangement to that at Exeter College, although it is broader in proportion and vaulted in timber rather than stone. The decoration and stained glass was the work of Clayton & Bell; the marble, mosaic and tile floor was by Burlison & Grylls. Although the college was expanding, this chapel might seem excessively large for its time – especially as compulsory attendance at chapel was abolished soon after its completion.

CAMBRIDGE, ST JOHN'S COLLEGE, MASTER'S LODGE

BELOW: The building of the grand new chapel and the extension of the hall at St John's required the demolition of the Master's Lodge as well as the old chapel. Scott designed a sumptuous new detached Master's Lodge overlooking gardens by the river Cam, which was built in 1863–65. George Gilbert Scott junior, who was an undergraduate at Jesus College at the time, seems to have assisted his busy father over the work at St John's and was surely instrumental in incorporating woodwork and other elements from the old lodge and chapel in the new Lodge as well as being responsible for decorative work.

HARROW SCHOOL, CHAPEL

LEFT: In 1854 Scott was invited to design a new chapel at Harrow School, to replace a smaller building of 1838 by Cockerell, by the headmaster, the Revd Dr Charles John. Vaughan, a pupil of Thomas Arnold's at Rugby. This contemporary print shows the nave with its circular piers and the wide south aisle, intended as a Crimean War memorial. The exterior is of flint and stone, with an apse overlooking the sloping ground to the east. The flèche was added in 1865 and the building later enlarged by Aston Webb.

HARROW SCHOOL, VAUGHAN LIBRARY

BELOW LEFT: The Vaughan Library, built in memory of the headmaster who unexpectedly retired in 1859, was built in 1861–63. It is a fine example of Scott's secular Gothic manner, built of polychromatic brick – in contrast to the more expensive stone and flint of the adjacent chapel, in accordance with Pugin's principle of 'propriety'. Lord Palmerston, an Old Harrovian, who had recently thwarted Scott over this Gothic design for the Foreign Office, laid the foundation stone. This photograph, taken in 2014, shows the symmetrical entrance front.

BELOW RIGHT: A detail of the gable above the central entrance, showing the fine decorative carving above the wheel window.

King's College London, Chapel

ABOVE: Scott was asked to replace the original first-floor chapel within Smirke's building for King's College London, because of its 'meagreness and poverty'. Along with his transmogrification of St Michael's Cornhill and his abortive neo-Byzantine design for the Government Offices, it is one of his few 'semi-classic' works. Because of its situation, he thought that 'in a classic building, the best mode of giving ecclesiastical character is the adoption of the form and, in some degree, the character of an ancient basilica'. As the raised floor could not take the weight of stone, Scott recommended 'double columns of metal (iron decorated with brass).' The Chapel was constructed in 1861–64, the original pitched roof being replaced by a flat ceiling in 1931–32 when more accommodation was created above. Photograph taken in 2006.

GLASGOW UNIVERSITY

LEFT: Glasgow University first proposed selling its old site in the High Street to a railway company and relocating to the more salubrious West End in 1845, when John Baird prepared designs. The project was revived in 1864 when Scott was appointed architect, without competition, for the proposed new buildings on top of Gilmorehill. This woodcut, published in the *Illustrated London News* in 1866, shows his accepted design in the style he initiated in Dundee: 'It is simply a thirteenth or fourteenth-century secular style with the addition of certain Scottish features, peculiar in that country to the sixteenth century, though in reality derived from the French style of the thirteenth and fourteenth centuries.'

LEFT: This photograph, by George Washington Wilson, shows Scott's University buildings after they were completed in 1870 but before the intended conical turret tops and the steeple over the central clock tower was completed to a shorter and lighter design with an openwork stone spire in 1886–88 by John Oldrid Scott.

BOMBAY UNIVERSITY

RIGHT: Scott was commissioned to design buildings for the new University of Bombay in 1864. They would be the finest among the series of magnificent Gothic revival buildings in the city facing Back Bay which were erected after the removal of the ramparts by the Governor, Sir Bartle Frere, in 1862. Unfortunately Scott's original design (now lost) greatly exceeded the funds available so he was informed, to his fury, in 1866 that 'the Syndicate had decided to avail itself of the experience of local architects for reducing the cost'. The University Library, with its glorious tall Rajabai Clock Tower, paid for by Premchand Roychund and completed in 1880 – seen here in a photograph of 2013 – seems to have been built essentially as Scott intended. He gave this landmark tower a 'look differing, so far as may be, from that of a church tower.'

RIGHT: Work began on building the modified University design in 1868. The climate of Bombay allowed Scott (and other architects) to indulge in the open arcades and open spiral staircases beloved of Gothicists in England which usually proved impractical in, say, London or Bradford. The Library, seen here in 2013, is built of tough roughly-dressed Kurla basalt and Porbanda stone; the interior is vaulted in timber. As Richard Butler has written Scott's Bombay University 'represents the most thorough statement of his distinctive secular Gothic style, despite his understandable dissatisfaction with the project … It is easily the most scholarly and most artistically successful example of Gothic Revival architecture in Bombay.' [134]

OPPOSITE: Scott's design for the Convocation Hall, mostly paid for by Sir Cowasjee Jehangir, would seem to have been the most altered by the local architects consulted, George Twigge-Molecey and Walter Paris, to reduce the cost. As built in 1869–74, the exterior, with its open spiral staircases and splendid rose window, was built of the same stone as the Library next door. Both are in the thirteenth-century Gothic manner characteristic of Scott. Photograph 2013.

LEFT: The interior of the Convocation Hall has an apsidal end behind the raised daïs. The galleries are supported on ornamental iron brackets which rest on elaborately carved corbels with elaborate heads carved, along with the rest of the sculpture, capitals and friezes, by Muccoond Ramchander and students at the J. J. School of Art in Bombay under the direction of John Lockwood Kipling. The stained glass was sent out from England and was made by Heaton, Butler & Bayne. Photograph 2014.

Rugby School House

LEFT: William Butterfield was responsible for the most conspicuous Victorian buildings at Rugby School, the public school reformed by Thomas Arnold, but Scott was responsible for one building. This is the first of new boarding houses owned by the school, built in 1852 and now called School Field. In the front facing the playing fields, built of diapered red brick, Scott delighted in a variety of Gothic window forms, disposed asymmetrically according to function. Photograph 2012.

Algarkirk, Lincoln, School

BELOW: Scott designed many small village schools. The one at Algarkirk in Lincolnshire is one of the most interesting. It was built of stone in 1856 and incorporated a house for the schoolmaster. Scott clearly enjoyed playing with the geometry of buttress and bellcote on the projecting porch bay. The school is now the village hall.

WALTON, SCHOOL

ABOVE: The school building in Walton village, Warwickshire, is a charming example of Scott's secular Gothic manner in red brick. An artful rustic porch is fitted in the recess between the school room and master's house.

COMMERCIAL

The great majority of Scott's commissions were from the Church of England, the government, town councils, educational and other institutions or private individuals, and he probably rather looked down on architects who specialised in commercial and speculative work. He was, however, responsible for one particularly fine Gothic bank, while what, today, is his best known and most celebrated building was commissioned by a railway company. The Midland Railway evidently wanted a well-known architect to design the hotel at its new London terminus at St Pancras and Scott was persuaded to enter a limited competition by a director whom he knew. His design was then chosen despite the fact that the estimated cost of his design greatly exceeded that specified in the brief. As a result, he was able to carry out a prominent work in the secular Gothic style he had intended for Whitehall until thwarted by Lord Palmerston. Scott was closely involved with this project and was responsible for the interiors of all the public spaces. But he was uncomfortably aware that the Midland Grand, with its rich and expensive Gothic detail derived from cathedral architecture, was really too grand and elaborate for a commercial hotel – 'too good for its purpose' – resulting in what J. T. Emmett called 'a complete travesty of noble associations'. That scarcely matters today, when Scott's hotel, magnificently restored, is so much admired and enjoyed.

LEEDS, BECKETT'S BANK
RIGHT: Atkinson Grimshaw painted this view of Park Row in 1882, with Scott's red brick Beckett's Bank the most conspicuous building. In 1959 Nikolaus Pevsner described this street, with buildings by Waterhouse, P. C. Hardwick and Lockwood & Mawson as well as Scott, as giving 'the full flavour of commercial Leeds'. Almost every building in this painting was demolished in the 1960s.

LEEDS, BECKETT'S BANK

LEFT: Beckett's Bank in Park Row in Leeds was a notable example of Scott's secular Gothic manner. Symmetrical, it sported both pointed and round arched windows, as recommended in Scott's book *Secular & Domestic Architecture*. It was built in 1863–67, with the local architect William P. Perkin looking after the interior. The bank was founded in Leeds in the eighteenth century by the Beckett family and was one source of the wealth of Scott's tormentor, Edmund Beckett Denison, later Sir Edmund Beckett. This building later become a branch of the Westminster Bank and was needlessly demolished in 1964 exactly a century after it was erected.

ST PANCRAS, MIDLAND GRAND HOTEL

RIGHT: Scott won the competition for the hotel to front the Midland Railway's new London terminus in 1865. This side elevation shows his original design, with the stupendous train shed by W. H. Barlow – the largest span in the world when completed in 1868 – encased in lower brick retaining walls and arcades in the Gothic style. As built, in two stages between 1868 and 1876, the Midland Grand Hotel would be less tall, with a whole storey eliminated.

ABOVE: This superb photograph of Scott's Midland Grand Hotel, was taken by Bedford Lemere in c.1880 soon after its completion in 1876. Scott noted that his commercial masterpiece 'was in the same style which I had almost originated several years earlier, for the government offices, but divested of the Italian element … It is often spoken of to me as the finest building in London …'

LEFT: The Midland Railway's booking hall was conveniently sited between the main station concourse and the carriage road leading from the tall departure arch penetrating the hotel. The Gothic theme continued in this tall space, lit from a lantern over a massive timber open hammerbeam roof. This structure, shown in this 1876 photograph, was badly damaged in an air raid by Gotha bombers in 1918 and replaced by a flat roof. Otherwise the interior survives today in use as a restaurant, the timber ticket office having been moved to the western side of the room.

LEFT: When it opened in 1873, the Midland Grand Hotel was the most modern and luxurious in the capital. It was, however, soon outclassed by newer establishments like the Savoy, equipped with hydraulic lifts and many more bathrooms – one reason why it closed as an hotel in 1935. This 1876 photograph shows the Ladies' Coffee Room, later the Ladies' Smoking Room, on the first floor above the entrance lobby. Its richly decorated interior, with lavish internal arcades, has now been restored.

BRIGHTON, BRILL'S BATHS

ABOVE: An unusual commission for Scott was for a swimming bath in Brighton. In 1866 Charles Brill decided to rebuild the town's first communal swimming bath, which had opened in 1823, and created a 65 ft diameter circular pool filled with seawater – the largest in Europe at the time. Scott demonstrated his happiness with iron structures by designing an iron and glass dome to go over this pool, which was enclosed within brick buildings in Scott's secular Gothic manner containing baths, changing rooms, a reading room and a billiard room. This photograph was taken shortly before the whole complex was demolished in 1929 and replaced by the Savoy Cinema.

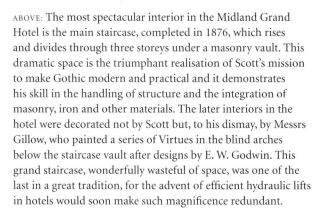

ABOVE: The most spectacular interior in the Midland Grand Hotel is the main staircase, completed in 1876, which rises and divides through three storeys under a masonry vault. This dramatic space is the triumphant realisation of Scott's mission to make Gothic modern and practical and it demonstrates his skill in the handling of structure and the integration of masonry, iron and other materials. The later interiors in the hotel were decorated not by Scott but, to his dismay, by Messrs Gillow, who painted a series of Virtues in the blind arches below the staircase vault after designs by E. W. Godwin. This grand staircase, wonderfully wasteful of space, was one of the last in a great tradition, for the advent of efficient hydraulic lifts in hotels would soon make such magnificence redundant.

DOMESTIC ARCHITECTURE

Scott designed many small houses as vicarages and parsonages, along with village schools, were often associated with the churches he designed. After the mid-1840s, as his reputation grew, rather grander clients began to come to him for larger houses. His first large country house was Alton Manor at Idridgehay in Derbyshire of 1846–47. Here – as with his early vicarages – Scott worked in the Tudor Gothic style, learning much from the work of Pugin. After the mid-1850s he began to experiment with the rather different secular Gothic manner based on the ideas he expounded in his book, *Remarks on Secular & Domestic Architecture, Present & Future*, in a small number of aristocratic country houses. However, despite the practical good sense of his theories, the results were somewhat ponderous and churchy in appearance. It must be admitted that Scott was not particularly skilled in the complex and demanding art of country house planning, and it is significant that such commissions seem to have dried up after the early 1860s. It was very much in reaction to the type of High Victorian country house, efficient rather than romantic, that Scott and his fellow Gothicists created that a younger generation – not least Scott's own two architect sons – turned to the 'Queen Anne' and 'Old English' styles in the 1870s in search of a prettier, more domestic-looking and less churchy manner of building. Discussing Scott's houses at Walton and Kelham, Goodhart-Rendel wrote that 'There is much in these buildings that at their date must have seemed commendable modern, and for that reason superior to the opportunistic compromise with archaeological Tudor offered by the school of Salvin; but their pitiful artistic inferiority to contemporary works by Scott's juniors … makes Scott's pretentions to leadership seem comical indeed.' And it is surely significant that not one of these large mansions houses is still lived in, though several now flourish as country house hotels.

NOTTINGHAMSHIRE, KELHAM HALL

RIGHT: This photograph shows the vaulted music hall at Kelham with its arcades and upper gallery as it looked in the 1960s. All the carving was carried out by W. G. Brindley of Farmer & Brindley; Scott thought it 'of a very high order'. From 1903 until 1974 Kelham was used by the Society of the Sacred Mission, which added a large and impressive neo-Byzantine chapel. After that the house served as the headquarters of Newark & Sherwood District Council but was sold in 2014 to Kelham Hall Ltd, which plans to open it as a luxury hotel and spa.

Haley Hill, Halifax, Vicarage

ABOVE: Scott designed a substantial vicarage to stand behind his 'best church', All Souls', Haley Hill, Halifax which was built at the same time. Scott's many such small houses were not standardised as variety was possible with the shape and placing of windows, the disposition of gables, bay windows and projecting bays. It is revealing to compare this with Scott's vicarage in Cambridge designed just a few years earlier.

Cambridge, St Paul's Vicarage

LEFT: Scott designed many vicarages. The one in Cambridge is not only representative but a definite product of his close personal attention because it was designed for his elder brother, the Revd John Scott, who was then the incumbent at St Paul's Church. Built in 1853–54 in red and yellow brick with diapering, the parsonage is characteristically asymmetrical and Puginian and has simplified Gothic windows and high-pitched gable-dormers.

WESTMINSTER, BROAD SANCTUARY HOUSES

ABOVE: This terrace of houses in Broad Sanctuary, Westminster, incorporating a gatehouse entrance to Dean's Yard were built in 1852–54 as an improvement soon after Victoria Street had been cut through the slums to the west of the Abbey. Scott, who was already Surveyor to the Abbey, probably owed this commission to the Sub-Dean, Lord John Thynne. The busy stone-faced front is a carefully asymmetrical composition while the crow-stepped gables combined with chimneys and turrets created 'the first truly dramatized roofscape in Victorian London'.[135] The rear elevation is of brick. This woodcut was published in *The Builder* in 1854.

RUGBY, BROWNSOVER HALL

BELOW LEFT: Brownsover Hall near Rugby, Warwickshire, was remodelled by Scott for John Ward-Boughton-Leigh. The work was completed in 1857. The exterior is of patterned brickwork and there is an impressive tower above the entrance. Photograph taken in 2012.

BELOW RIGHT: The interior of Brownsover Hall is more satisfactory than the exterior. This view, taken in 2012, shows the staircase hall and upper gallery. There is the open arcade, with marble columns, that Scott liked and an impressive wall of rational Gothic fenestration beyond. Having been the residence of Sir Frank Whittle, inventor of the jet engine, Brownsover Hall is now a hotel and restaurant.

DORKING, PIPPBROOK HOUSE

ABOVE: Scott was asked to remodel Pippbrook House on the edge of Dorking, Surrey, by William Henry Forman, iron merchant and landowner, who had paid for the south chancel chapel in Scott's rebuilding of St George's, Doncaster. In 1856–58 the older house was refaced and Gothicised. There is no denying that the composition of Pippbrook House is unsatisfactory and awkward, though Ian Nairn perhaps went too far in describing it as 'Very ugly: the ugliness of carelessness and insensitivity, not of protest'.[136] Photograph 2010.

LEFT: Scott added a new and rather coarse lower museum wing to the rear of Pippbrook House to contain Forman's collection of antiquities and art. These are long dispersed, but some good chimney pieces and decorative work survives internally. Now owned by Mole Valley Council, the house served for many years as a public library.

NOTTINGHAMSHIRE, KELHAM HALL

ABOVE: Scott delivered the first two chapters of what would become his influential book, *Remarks on Secular & Domestic Architecture*, as a lecture at Newark-on-Trent in 1855. This may well have brought him to the attention of J. H. Manners-Sutton, who asked him to make improvements to his Nottinghamshire seat, Kelham Hall. In 1857 the house was largely destroyed by fire and in 1858 Scott prepared his design for rebuilding. Work began the following year. In this house Scott was able to carry out his ideas about a modern domestic Gothic architecture, availing itself of all modern improvements. This view of the east front of Kelham Hall is taken from the *County Seats of the Noblemen and Gentlemen of Great Britain and Ireland* by F. O. Morris, published in 1870.

LEFT: This view of the west front of Kelham Hall, taken in 1997, shows the modernity of Scott's approach. His book argued that in a modern Gothic, windows need not be pointed, so here they are square-headed, incorporating the boon of plate-glass. The only conventionally Gothic windows mark the interior position of the chapel. But although Scott's approach rejected the romantic antiquarianism of early nineteenth-century country houses, whether Jacobean, Tudor or castellated, the result at Kelham, expensively and substantially built, does not look very domestic.

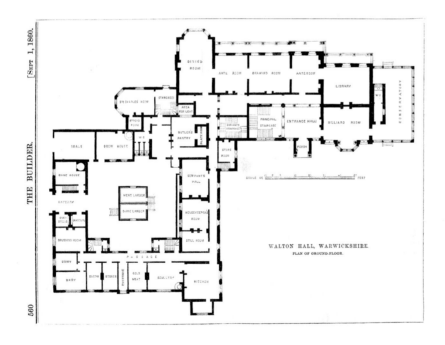

[Sept 1, 1860.

THE BUILDER.

560]

WALTON HALL, WARWICKSHIRE.
PLAN OF GROUND-FLOOR.

WARWICKSHIRE, WALTON HALL.

ABOVE: Scott remodelled Walton Hall, Warwickshire, for Sir Charles Mordaunt, Bart, in 1858–62. Scott wrote that 'In domestic architecture I do think that I struck out a variety [of Gothic] eminently practical, and thoroughly suited to the wants and habits of the day' and that Walton Hall 'contains it in a minor form …' This woodcut, after a drawing by J. D. Wyatt, was published in *The Builder* in 1860.

LEFT: Only some of the walls of the previous Walton Hall were retained and Scott had a comparatively free hand in planning the new mansion, as shown in this plate published in *The Builder* in 1860. The principal reception rooms face the southern aspect behind a continuous open arcade. Scott was also able to plan a generous service wing around a courtyard.

ABOVE: Walton Hall is perhaps the most sympathetic of Scott's country houses. The elevations are more disciplined and it is built of a beautiful local white lias stone with dressings of Bath stone, while the roof is covered in green and blue slates. Photograph 2012.

ABOVE: The entrance front of Walton Hall shows the successful application of the ideas expounded in Scott's 1857 book. There is plate glass in square-headed windows and the arch over the point is semi-circular rather than pointed. It was in front of this new house that one of the great Victorian sex scandals began, when, in 1868, Mordaunt returned from a fishing trip in Norway to find the Prince of Wales showing his new young wife how to drive a carriage and pair. The heir to the throne left rapidly, Mordaunt ordered the horses to be shot and initiated divorce proceedings, the unfortunate Lady Mordaunt eventually being confined to an asylum.

LEFT: The staircase hall at Walton is particularly impressive, with arcades with marble columns on two floors and an upper gallery. This photograph was taken in the 1970s when the house was an hotel – as it is today.

DENBIGHSHIRE, HAFODUNOS HOUSE

LEFT: Hafodunos at Llangernyw in Denbighshire was Scott's last country house and arguably his most succesful. He completely rebuilt the existing house in 1861–66 for the Liverpool merchant and shipowner, Samuel Sandbach. The walls were of patterned brickwork and, as at Kelham, there was a clock tower with a spire. The conservatory was added in 1883 by John Oldrid Scott. Hafodunos was gutted by local arsonists in 2004 and now stands as a forlorn ruin. This photograph was taken in 1954.

KENT, LEE PRIORY

BELOW: Lee Priory in Kent was originally a Gothic house by James Wyatt built in 1785 and described by Horace Walpole as 'a child of Strawberry, prettier than the parent'. The refacing in patterned brick and the extensions of 1861 designed by Scott were not so pretty, and such serious-minded insensitivity was a typical expression of the disdain the Victorians felt towards the early non-archaeological and less ponderous phase of the Gothic Revival. This photograph was taken in 1953 shortly before the whole house was demolished the following year.

RESTORATIONS

Church and cathedral restoration formed a very large part of Scott's practice, but such jobs are difficult to illustrate without pictorial and archaeological evidence of the appearance of ancient buildings before he turned his attention to them. The examples given here are therefore those where Scott made a significant impact on the appearance of the building, as with Ely Cathedral and Westminster Abbey, and those in which the new furnishings he designed are conspicuous and interesting. This is the case with several cathedrals entrusted to his care, particularly those in which Scott designed a new open screen as part of his rearrangement and refurnishing of the choir. Certain cathedrals, such as Ely and Lichfield, show both Scott's skill and sensitivity as a restorer of Medieval buildings and his notable ability to design appropriate but imaginative new furnishings to make them suitable for modern worship. In the ecclesiastical sphere, these cathedrals show Scott at his very best, both as a Medieval scholar and as a designer.

LICHFIELD CATHEDRAL

RIGHT: Scott's restoration of Lichfield Cathedral, where he had to repair much damage caused by Wyatt, was one of his best and most sympathetic, and the superb new furnishings he introduced have survived the anti-Victorian prejudice of the mid-twentieth century. He wrote that, 'I erected an altar-screen on the site of the ancient one, and put up a metal screen between the choir and the nave. No old stalls remaining, new ones were introduced …' This photograph shows Scott's magnificent screen.

Stafford, St Mary's

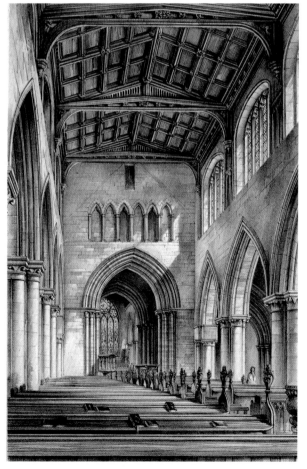

ABOVE: St Mary's Stafford was Scott's first important restoration, carried out in 1842–45. The lithographs from drawings by John Masfen published in the lavish book of 1852 about the restoration must here be representative of Scott's intentions in the many, many restorations of churches he carried out. This view of the exterior shows the south transept Scott rebuilt and the pinnacles replaced on the crossing tower while leaving alone the Perpendicular clerestory and battlements.

LEFT: Inside the church, Scott cleared away galleries and other later fittings and reseated the nave with new benches.

Ely Cathedral

RIGHT: Ely was Scott's first cathedral. He was appointed in 1847 and worked there over the next two decades. His most conspicuous intervention externally was the recreation of the original appearance of the lantern of the Octagon, which 'I most carefully investigated from ancient evidences, and can speak of most of it with much certainty'.

BELOW RIGHT: Scott moved the Medieval stalls into the choir just east of the Octagon. Here he installed his first new open screen, this one of timber. In this nineteenth-century photograph, looking west, the organ case was by Scott and he was instrumental in having the nave ceiling decorated by Henry Le Strange and Thomas Gambier Parry.

BELOW: In this 1998 view looking east in the choir, the reredos, gasoliers (by Skidmore) and the tile and marble floor were all designed by Scott.

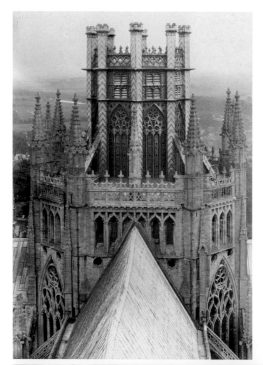

WESTMINSTER ABBEY

ABOVE LEFT: Scott was made Surveyor to Westminster Abbey in 1849, 'a great and lasting source of delight.' He was responsible for rescuing and restoring the thirteenth-century Chapter House from a state of utter degradation. In the 2014 photograph, the window tracery and the high pitched roof, as well as the pinnacles on the south transept towers, are all due to Scott.

ABOVE RIGHT: Inside the Chapter House, Scott was responsible for exposing the Medieval sculpture, wall paintings and tiles. Some new work had to be introduced. This trumeau above the double doorway showing Christ in Majesty was carved by James Redfern.

LEFT: Amongst the new furnishings Scott introduced to the Abbey, the most prominent was once the nave pulpit, since removed, in front of which Scott would be buried.

OPPOSITE: Scott's last work at the Abbey was the recovery of the original design of the portals of the North Transept. This photograph of c.1880 shows the restoration of these portals, largely carried out after his death by J. O. Scott, nearing completion. The upper part of the transept would be 'restored' and gratuitously altered by Scott's successor, J. L. Pearson, in the 1880s.

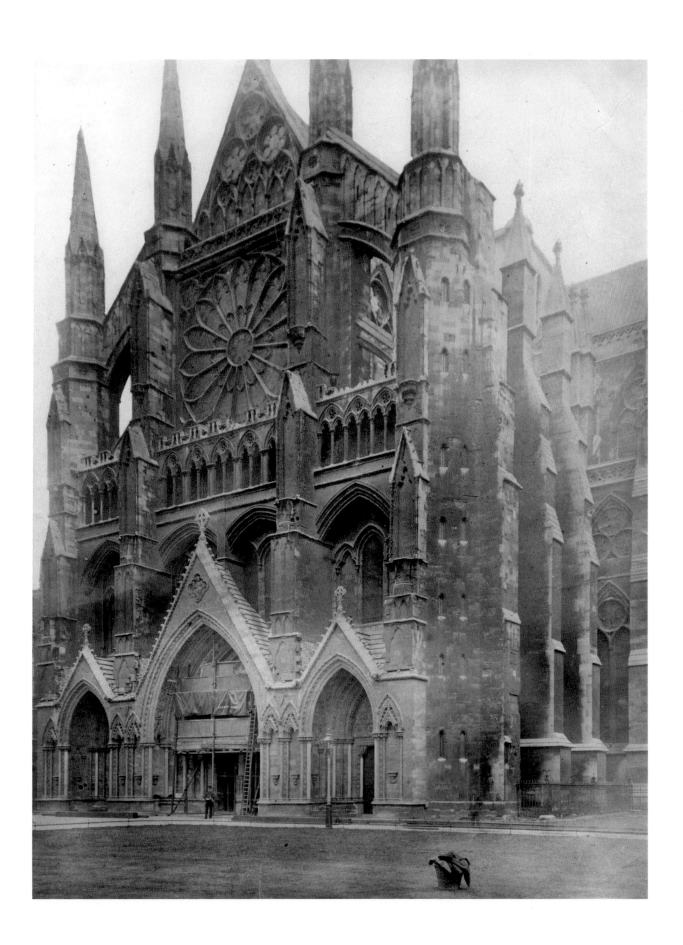

SALISBURY CATHEDRAL

ABOVE: At Salisbury Cathedral, where he was appointed in 1859, Scott strengthened the precarious crossing tower and spire as well as undoing some of the damage perpetrated by Wyatt. In this nineteenth-century photograph, the open metal choir screen (by Skidmore) and the reredos beyond were both introduced by Scott and both were thrown out in the 1960s. His pulpit has survived, however, and the cross over the screen is now at the Victoria & Albert Museum.

HEREFORD CATHEDRAL

LEFT: Scott's finest and most elaborate cathedral screen, made by Francis Skidmore, was designed for Hereford Cathedral. Before it was installed, Skidmore requested that it be exhibited at the International Exhibition of 1862 held in South Kensington, where it was much admired. This lithographed plate is from *Masterpieces of Industrial Art and Sculpture at the International Exhibition, 1862* by J. B. Waring.

RIGHT: This nineteenth-century photograph shows the Scott-Skidmore screen in situ at Hereford Cathedral. Scott later confessed that 'Skidmore followed my design, but somewhat aberrantly. It is a fine work, but too loud and self-asserting for an English church.' It was taken out in 1966 and is now on display in the Victoria & Albert Museum in London.

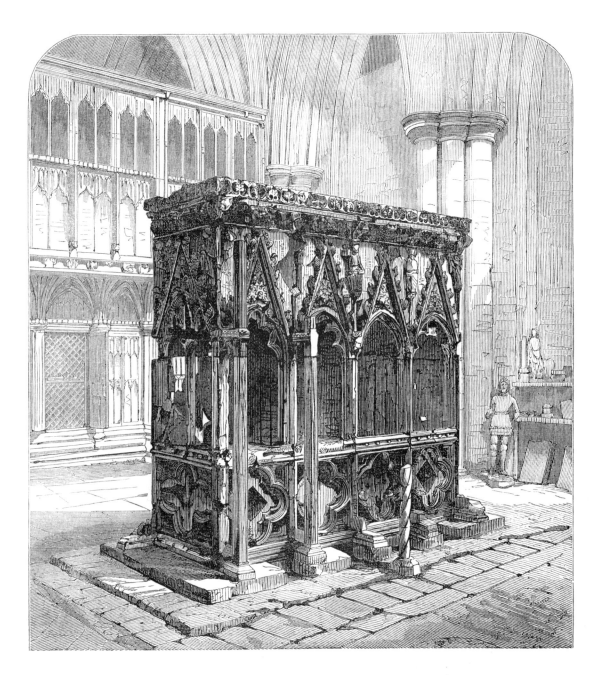

St Albans Abbey: Shrine of St Alban.

ABOVE: Scott worked extensively at St Albans, shoring up the crossing tower and correcting the lean of the south wall of the nave. Towards the end, Scott had to endure the interference of Lord Grimthorpe, who did terrible things to the Abbey Church – elevated to cathedral status in 1877 – when Scott was safely out of the way. One of Scott's proudest achievements was to recreate from fragments the fourteenth-century marble shrine of St Alban, which was, 'by the ingenuity of the foreman and the clerk of works, set up again, exactly in its old place, stone for stone, fragment for fragment: the most marvellous restitution that was ever made.' This woodcut of the restored shrine was published in the *Illustrated London News* in 1873.

London, St Michael's, Cornhill

OPPOSITE: Very different was Scott's treatment of Wren's City Church of St Michael's, Cornhill, where he 'attempted, by the use of a sort of early Basilican style, to give tone to the existing classic architecture'. This he did in 1857–60 by placing Lombardic tracery within Wren's simple windows and richly decorating the interior, thus showing rather less respect for the work of the seventeenth century than he usually did for the Medieval. Most of the decoration has since been removed, but his fine furnishings survive. Scott also added a Gothic porch to the early eighteenth-century Gothic tower.

ENVOI

To appreciate the versatility of which George Gilbert Scott was capable and the beauty and charm of his work at its best, there is no better place to visit than Clifton Hampden in Oxfordshire where, thanks to the munificence of the Gibbs family, he restored the church, added to the village school, built a new parsonage – really a small country house – and designed a new bridge to cross the River Thames. The moving force and benefactor was Henry Huck Gibbs (whose uncle William built Tyntesfield in Somerset and was one of the founders of Keble College). Scott restored and enlarged the ruinous church, dramatically sited on a bluff above the river, in two phases. The first was in 1843–44, after which Scott wrote to Edward Freeman that 'I have lately been doctoring up rather than restoring a little church at Clifton Hampden … we had very little left to restore.' The second was in 1864–67, directed by his former pupil Charles Buckeridge, when a fine open metal screen was installed embellished with figures of St Michael and All Angels by James Redfern.

CLIFTON HAMPDEN, ST MICHAEL AND ALL ANGELS
RIGHT: The Church of St Michael and All Angels at Clifton Hampden, seen from the riverbank in 2014. The charming bellcote and all that is visible here is due to Scott, although the lych gate is later.

ABOVE: The interior of St Michael and All Angels in 2014: the arcades are ancient but everything else (except the later reredos by Buckeridge) is by Scott. In the chancel is an elaborate canopied tomb, designed by Scott, for the 'refounder' of the church, George Henry Gibbs. The screen was made not, for once, by Skidmore but by Hart & Son.

LEFT: Next to the church, Scott built in 1843–46 a new Parsonage in Tudor Gothic overlooking the Thames. It was enlarged by Scott in 1864–65. This fine house was bought back in 1905 by the 2nd Baron Aldenham, the son of H. H. Gibbs, and renamed the Manor House. In this view, taken in 2014 from the churchyard, the chimney to the left of the bay window has been truncated.

ABOVE: Scott designed a toll bridge to replace the ferry across the Thames. Built of brick, made nearby, in 1864, it was paid for by H. H. Gibbs. The arches, of course, are pointed, as in ancient bridges. As Scott wrote at the very end of his life, recalling his conversion to the Gothic cause decades earlier, 'every aspiration of my heart had become mediaeval'.

REFERENCES

As extensive quotations are made from Scott's *Personal and Professional Recollections*, both the original MS and the published volume, page references are not given here.

1 Quoted in G. Gilbert Scott, ed., *Personal and Professional Recollections by the late Sir George Gilbert Scott, R.A.* (London, 1879), p. 388.
2 G. A. Cate, ed., *The Correspondence of Thomas Carlyle and John Ruskin* (Stanford, 1982), p. 180.
3 Anthea Jones, *Tewkesbury Abbey: The Victorian Restoration Controversy* (Much Wenlock, 2012), p. 2.
4 *Transactions of the Royal Institute of British Architects*, 1878–9, p. 204.
5 M. S. Briggs, 'Sir Gilbert Scott, R.A.' in the *Architectural Review* xxiv, 1908, p. 147.
6 W. R. Lethaby, *Westminster Abbey and the King's Craftsmen* (London, 1906), pp. 83, 45.
7 Quoted by Briggs, *Architectural Review*, p. 147.
8 Quoted in Scott, *Recollections*, p. 384.
9 Alexander Thomson, 'An inquiry . . . with some remarks on Mr. Scott's plans', 1866, reprinted in Gavin Stamp, ed., *The Light of Truth and Beauty: The Lectures of Alexander 'Greek' Thomson, Architect, 1817–1875* (Glasgow, 1999).
10 Loch and Maclaurin to subcommittee 14 September 1864 and minutes, quoted in Nick Haynes, *Building Knowledge: An Architectural History of the University of Glasgow* (Edinburgh and Glasgow, 2013), p. 56.
11 Basil H. Jackson, ed., *Recollections of Thomas Graham Jackson* (Oxford, 1950), p. 59, (see also Sir Nicholas Jackson, Bt, ed., *Recollections. The Life and Travels of a Victorian Architect, Sir Thomas Graham Jackson Bt R.A.* (London, 2003), p. 57).
12 W. R. Lethaby, *Philip Webb and his Work* (Oxford, 1935), p. 66.
13 Charles L. Eastlake, *A History of the Gothic Revival* (London, 1872), p. 296.
14 James Fergusson, revised Robert Kerr, *History of the Modern Styles of Architecture* (London, 1891), 3rd ed, vol. II, pp. 416–17.
15 John T. Emmett, 'The State of English Architecture', *Quarterly Review*, April 1872 and in Emmett, *Six Essays* (London, 1891), pp. 10, 16.
16 Emmett, *Quarterly Review*, p. 33.
17 Jackson, *Recollections of Thomas Graham Jackson*, p. 153.
18 *The Times*, 28 March 1878; *The Builder* xxxvi, 1878; *British Architect* ix, 1878, p. 155.
19 Briggs, *Architectural Review*, pp. 92, 152, 182.
20 Kenneth Clark, *The Gothic Revival: An essay in the history of taste* (London, 1928), p. 230.
21 A. E. Richardson, 'Architecture', in G. M. Young, ed., *Early Victorian England 1830–1865* (London, 1934), vol. II, pp. 226–7.
22 John W. Dodds, *The Age of Paradox: a biography of England 1841–1851* (London, 1953), p. 266.
23 Turnor, *Nineteenth Century Architecture in Britain* (London, 1950), p. 80.
24 Basil F. L. Clarke, *Church Builders of the Nineteenth Century* (London, 1938), p. 172.
25 John Betjeman, *First and Last Loves* (London, 1952), p. 136.
26 H. S. Goodhart-Rendel, *English Architecture since the Regency* (London, 1953), pp. 95–6.
27 *The Victorian Society Report 1963–1964*, p. 8.
28 Candida Lycett-Green, ed., *John Betjeman Letters, volume two, 1951 to 1984* (London 1995), p. 319.
29 Sir John Summerson, 'Red Elephant in the Euston Road' in the *Illustrated London News* ccli, October 1967, p. 18.
30 The *Guardian*, 8 July 2011, p. 35.
31 Simon Heffer, *High Minds: The Victorians and the Birth of Modern Britain* (London, 2013), p. 347.
32 Nikolaus Pevsner, *The Buildings of England, Wiltshire* (Harmondsworth, 2nd ed 1975), p. 409; *Staffordshire* (Harmondsworth, 1974), p. 186.
33 *Daily Telegraph*, 15 March 1993.
34 Photocopy of typescript by Stephen Dykes Bower, 1978.
35 John Betjeman, *London's Historic Railway Stations* (London, 1972), p. 14.
36 Original MS at the Royal Commission for the Ancient and Historical Monuments of Scotland, published in full in Gavin Stamp, 'In Search of the Byzantine: George Gilbert Scott's Diary of an Architectural Tour in France in 1862' in *Architectural History: the Journal of the Society of Architectural Historians of Great Britain* xli, 2003, pp. 215, 211, 205, 218.
37 *Architectural History* 19, 1976.
38 *The Builder*, 7 June 1879; *RIBA Transactions*, 1879, p. 199.
39 *The Builder*, 7 June 1879, p. 645.
40 Gavin Stamp, 'The Hungerford Market' in *AA Files* 11, Spring 1986.
41 For Roberts, and for the Camberwell Collegiate School, see James Stevens Curl, *The Life and Work of Henry Roberts 1803–1876* (Chichester, 1983), p. 16, ff.
42 Jackson, *Recollections of Thomas Graham Jackson*, p. 51.
43 Kathryn Morrison, *The Workhouse: A Study of Poor-Law Buildings in England* (Swindon, 1999), p. 71, ff; Kathryn A. Morrison, 'The New-Poor-Law workhouses of George Gilbert Scott and William Bonython Moffatt' in *Architectural History* 40, 1997, pp. 184–203.
44 Quoted in Michael Fisher, *Pugin-Land* (Stafford, 2002), p. 119.
45 Scott to General Grey 20 December 1869, quoted in Gavin Stamp, 'George Gilbert Scott, the Memorial Competition, and the Critics', in Chris Brooks, ed., *The Albert Memorial* (New Haven and London, 2000), p. 113.
46 Rosemary Hill, *God's Architect: Pugin and the Building of Romantic Britain* (London, 2007), p. 363.
47 See H. F. Mallgrave, *Gottfried Semper: Architect of the Nineteenth Century* (New Haven and London, 1996), p. 137 ff.
48 Edward A. Freeman, *A History of Architecture* (London, 1849), p. 452.
49 Michael J. Lewis, *The Politics of the German Gothic Revival: August Reichensperger* (New York and Cambridge? 1993), p. 1.
50 *The Ecclesiologist* iv, 1845, p. 184.
51 The letter was printed, in full, in Scott, *Recollections*; in the original MS he wrote 'see my defence it is lithographed and I have some copies'.
52 Quoted in a memoir of his father by Charles Hilbert Strange, MS in RIBA library.
53 It was from this union that Elisabeth Scott, the architect of the Shakespeare Memorial Theatre at Stratford-upon-Avon, won in competition in 1928, was descended.
54 F. M. Simpson, 'George Frederick Bodley, R.A., F.S.A., D.C.L.' in *RIBA Journal*, p. 145; Edward Warren, 'The Life and Work of George Frederick Bodley' in *RIBA Journal*, 1910, p. 306.
55 Jackson, *op. cit.*, 2003, prints a letter from Scott, dated 7th November 1861, about Jackson's further architectural education, recommending four principal classes of study: 1, artistic skill and knowledge, including drawing at the Architectural Museum, 2, knowledge of actual architecture, in which 'Classical architecture, I fear, must have its due attention...', 3, practical knowledge, and, 4, literary knowledge or architecture.
56 *The Builder*, 6 April 1878, p. 339.
57 David Cole, *The Work of Sir Gilbert Scott* (London, 1980), p. 67.
58 George Gilbert Scott, *A Plea for the Faithful Restoration of our Ancient Churches* (Oxford, 1850), p. 87.
59 Eastlake, pp. 294–5; Geoffrey Tyack, *Oxford: an architectural guide* (Oxford, 1998), p. 225.
60 *Building News*, 19 April 1878.
61 Simpson, *RIBA Journal*, p. 146.
62 Aidan Whelan, 'George Gilbert Scott: A Pioneer of Constructional Polychromy?' in *Architectural History* 57, 2014, pp. 217–38.

63 Nikolaus Pevsner, *The Buildings of England: Staffordshire* (Harmondsworth, 1974), p. 261.

64 Scott, *A Plea*, pp. 111–12.

65 Nikolaus Pevsner, *The Buildings of England, Yorkshire: The West Riding* (Harmondsworth, 1959), p. 527.

66 The late John Masfen, junior, *Views of the Church of St. Mary at Stafford* (London, 1852), pp. 20–1.

67 Scott, *A Plea*, pp. 24–5, 20–1, 33, 35.

68 Suzanna Branfoot, 'A Plea for the Faithful Restoration of our Ancient Churches': A re-appraisal of the restoration and conservation of mediaeval churches and cathedrals by George Gilbert Scott, PhD thesis for the University of Reading, 2004, p. 252.

69 Copy from Roy Davids Ltd, 2000.

70 *Consecration versus Desecration:* 'An Appeal to the Lord Bishop of London against the Bill for the Destruction of City Churches and the Sale of Burial Grounds' (London, 1854), pp. 24–5.

71 *The Times*, 23 April 1878.

72 Papers Read at the Royal Institute of British Architects, vol. xii, 1861–2, p. 71.

73 *Illustrated London News*, 29 September 1855, p. 398.

74 Branfoot, 'A Plea . . .': A re-appraisal, pp. 94, 170.

75 Quoted in Ingrid Brown, 'The Hereford Screen' in *Ecclesiology Today* 47, 48, July 2013, p. 3.

76 Benedict Read, *Victorian Sculpture* (New Haven and London, 1982), p. 266.

77 Brian Hanson, '*Labor ipse voluptas*: Scott, Street, Ruskin, and the Value of Work' in R. Daniels and G. Brandwood, eds, *Ruskin and Architecture* (Reading, 2003), p. 135; *ex info.* Rosemary Hill.

78 Quoted by Read, *Victorian Sculpture*, p. 266.

79 George Gilbert Scott, *Remarks on Secular and Domestic Architecture, Present and Future* (London, 1857), pp.vii–viii, 262, 35, 107–9.

80 Scott, *Remarks*, pp. 188, 259–60.

81 Mark Girouard, *The Victorian Country House* (Oxford, 1971), p. 108.

82 See Elizabeth Hamilton, *The Warwickshire Scandal* (Norwich, 1999).

83 Quoted in Ian Toplis, *The Foreign Office: An architectural history* (London, 1987), p. 200.

84 Hansard (Commons), quoted in Cole, *The Work of Sir Gilbert Scott*, p. 76.

85 Quoted in Toplis, *The Foreign Office*, p. 85.

86 Quoted in Toplis, *The Foreign Office*, p. 96.

87 Ruskin to Eneas Sweetland Dallas, 10 September 1859, quoted in Michael W. Brooks, *John Ruskin and Victorian Architecture* (New Brunswick and London, 1987), p. 155.

88 *The Gothic Renaissance: Its Origin, Progress and Principles*, reprinted from the *Constitutional Press Magazine* (London, 1860).

89 Quoted in Toplis, *The Foreign Office*, p. 164.

90 Jackson, *Recollections of Thomas Graham Jackson*, p. 73.

91 *Building News*, 28 June 1867, p. 435.

92 *The Times*, 2 July 1872, p. 12; Brooks, ed., *The Albert Memorial*, p. 128.

93 Richard Butler, 'George Gilbert Scott and the University of Bombay' in *The Victorian*: the magazine of the Victorian Society 37, July 2011, pp.10–13.

94 See Angus Trumble, 'Gilbert Scott's "bold and beautiful experiment"' in *Burlington Magazine*, vol. 141, December 1999 and vol. 142, January 2000.

95 Scott, *A Plea*, p. 115.

96 Quoted in G. A. Bremner, *Imperial Gothic: Religious Architecture and High Anglican Culture in the British Empire c. 1840–1870* (New Haven and London, 2013), p. 103.

97 Bremner, *Imperial Gothic*, p. xiii.

98 Cole, *The Work of Sir Gilbert Scott*, p. 124.

99 *Transactions of the Royal Institute of British Architects*, 1878, p. 204.

100 *Glasgow Herald*, 8 November 1870.

101 Sam McKinstry, 'Business Success and the Architectural Practice of Sir George Gilbert Scott, c. 1875–1878: a Study in Weberian Motivation, Sound Management and Networks of Trust',

University of the West of Scotland Working Paper prepared in connection with Leverhulme Trust Project.

102 Jackson, *Recollections of Thomas Graham Jackson*, p. 61.

103 Scott to J. D. Wyatt, 19 June 1867, by courtesy of Julian Browning.

104 *Builders Journal and Architectural Record*, 30 May 1900, quoted in Andrew Saint, *The Image of the Architect* (New Haven and London, 1983), p. 68.

105 *The Times*, 29 December 1870.

106 Jackson, *Recollections of Thomas Graham Jackson*, p. 50.

107 RIBA Transactions 1878, p. 204

108 *The British Architect and Northern Engineer*, 5 April 1878, p. 155.

109 Jackson, *Recollections of Thomas Graham Jackson*, pp. 58–61.

110 Sir Geo. Gilbert Scott, RA, ed., *Family Prayers by the late Mrs Geo. Gilbert Scott* (London, 1873).

111 Gavin Stamp, 'The Photograph Album of Albert Henry Scott, the photographer son of George Gilbert Scott' in *The Antiquaries Journal*, the journal of the Society of Antiquaries of London, vol. 93, 2013, pp. 401–15.

112 Notes in a sketchbook, recorded in Julian Litten, 'The Life of Sir Gilbert Scott' in Roger Dixon, ed., *Sir Gilbert Scott and the Scott Dynasty* (London 1980), p. 14.

113 *The Bury and Norwich Post, and Suffolk Herald*, 22 November 1870.

114 Melville Scott, *The Force of Love: being a memoir of the Ven. Melville Horne Scott, M.A., Archdeacon of Stafford and Residentiary Canon of Lichfield Cathedral* (Derby and London 1899), pp. 297–8.

115 Sir Gilbert Scott, RA, *Lectures on the Rise and Development of Mediaeval Architecture Delivered at the Royal Academy* (London, 1879), vol. II, p. 229.

116 *The Spectator*, 27 February 1875.

117 *Transactions of the Royal Institute of British Architects*, 1873–4 vol 24, pp. 7-11.

118 quoted in Michael W. Brooks, *John Ruskin and Victorian Architecture* (New Brunswick and London, 1987), p. 273.

119 *Transactions of the Royal Institute of British Architects*, vol 25 1874–5, pp. 1-13.

120 *Transactions of the Royal Institute of British Architects*, vol 26 1875–6, pp. 2-20.

121 *The Builder*, 2 June 1877, p. 552.

122 Last Will and Testament of Sir Gilbert Scott, dated 28 November 1876.

123 J. O. Scott to J. T. Irvine, 18 April 1878, 22 April 1880 [RCAHMS].

124 G. G. Scott to J. T. Irvine, 24 February 1881 [RCAHMS].

125 Michael Hall, *George Frederick Bodley and the Later Gothic Revival in Britain and America* (New Haven & London, 2014), p.28.

126 John Betjeman, *First and Last Loves* (London, 1952), p.188.

127 H. S. Goodhart-Rendel, *Journal of the London Society*, November 1958, p.45.

128 Ian Nairn & Nikolaus Pevsner, The Buildings of England: Surrey (Harmondsworth, 1962), p.427.

129 Nikolaus Pevsner, *The Buildings of England: Yorkshire the West Riding*, 1959), p.181.

130 Quoted in Michael Barney, *The Archdeacon and the Architect* (London, 1972), p.5.

131 G. A. Bremner, 'Scott and the Wider World: The Colonial Cathedrals, 1846–74' in P. S. Barnwell, Geoffrey Tyack & William Whyte, *George Gilbert Scott, 1811–1878: An Architect and his Influence* (Donington, 2014), p.71.

132 A. W. N. Pugin, *A letter on the proposed protestant memorial …* (London, 1839).

133 quoted in Geoffrey Tyack, 'Scott in Oxford' in Barnwell &c., 2014, *op.cit.*, p.118.

134 Butler, Bombay, *op.cit.*, p.13.

135 Simon Bradley & Nikolaus Pevsner, *The Buildings of England: London 6 Westminster* (New Haven & London, 2003), p.277.

136 Nairn, *Surrey, op. cit.*, p.168.

INDEX

Page numbers *in italics* refer to
illustrations.

SELECT BIBLIOGRAPHY

Scott was a 'confirmed scribbler' and he wrote a great deal, usually while travelling: letters, reports on buildings, his recollections, articles, lectures, letters to *The Times*, and more. Much of this material was published, in journals or newspapers or as printed reports or pamphlets, but cannot all be listed here. Indeed, a comprehensive Scott bibliography would be difficult to compile. The books he published were as follows: *A Plea for the Faithful Restoration of our Ancient Churches* (1850); *Remarks on Secular and Domestic Architecture, Present and Future* (1857, second edition 1858); *Gleanings from Westminster Abbey* (with others, 1861, expanded edition 1863); and, posthumously, *Lectures on the Rise and Development of Mediaeval Architecture* (2 vols, 1879) and *Personal and Professional Recollections...* edited by G.G. Scott junior (1879; new edition, with complete text, edited by Gavin Stamp, Stamford, 1995).

Although there are few published studies of his whole life and work, there is a vast literature on Scott's architecture in the form of articles (not least the obituaries) in contemporary periodicals - *The Builder*, the *Building News*, *The Ecclesiologist*, the *Civil Engineer's and Architect's Journal*, *The British Architect*, the *Illustrated London News*, and the *Transactions of the Royal Institute of British Architects*, etc. – as well more recent studies of individual buildings such as guides to churches (there are two monographs devoted to the Albert Memorial, two on the Foreign Office and three on St Pancras) and, not least, the entries in the *Buildings of England* series commenced by Nikolaus Pevsner. All these, again, cannot be listed here, although some useful publications are cited in the references to the text. The more general studies on or concerning Scott are as follows: Martin S. Briggs 'Sir Gilbert Scott, R.A.' (four articles in the *Architectural Review*, 1908); *Sir Gilbert Scott (1811-1878): Architect of the Gothic Revival* (catalogue of the exhibition at the Victoria & Albert Museum, 1978); Roger Dixon, ed., *Sir Gilbert Scott and the Scott Dynasty*, (South Bank Architectural Papers, 1980); David Cole, *The Work of Sir Gilbert Scott* (including an invaluable comprehensive list of works: Architectural Press, London, 1980); Geoffrey Fisher, Gavin Stamp & others, Joanna Heseltine, ed., *The Scott Family: Catalogue of the Drawings Collection of the Royal Institute of British Architects* (Gregg International, Amersham, 1981); Ian Toplis, *The Foreign Office: An architectural history* (Mansell, London & New York, 1987); M.H. Port, *Imperial London: Civil Government Building in London 1850-1915* (Yale University Press, New Haven & London, 1995); Chris Brooks, ed., *The Albert Memorial. The Prince Consort National Memorial: its History, Contexts, and Conservation* (Yale University Press, New Haven & London, 2000); Simon Bradley, *St Pancras Station* (Profile Books, London, 2007 & 2011); and the latest: P.S. Barnwell, Geoffrey Tyack & William Whyte, eds, *Sir George Gilbert Scott, 1811-1878*, with contributions by Gavin Stamp. Chris Miele, Geoff Brandwood, G.A. Bremner, Claudia Marx, Geoffrey Tyack, Simon Bradley, Peter Howell, M.H. Port, Kimberley Frost & William Whyte (Shaun Tyas, Donington, 2014). There is also a very useful unpublished Ph.D thesis by Suzanna Branfoot on Scott's restorations of churches and cathedrals and an unpublished typescript for a proposed book on Scott by the late Ian Toplis.

ACKNOWLEDGEMENTS

Many historians, fellow members of the Victorian Society and others are, naturally, interested in Scott and in writing this book I have benefitted from help by and information from Simon Bradley, Steven Brindle, Mosette Broderick, Julian Browning, Richard Butler, Donald Buttress, James Franks, Michael Hall, Craig Hamilton, Edmund Harris, Michael Hoare, Peter Howell, the late Paul Joyce, Sam McKinstry, Kenneth Powell, Andrew Saint, Peter Taylor, Angus Trumble and Michael Whittaker, amongst others. In addition, over many years, I have enjoyed the help and kindness of Richard Gilbert Scott, who inherited much precious material about his great-grandfather. As regards institutions, I should like to thank the staff of the RIBA Drawings Collection, past and present; Ian Leith, the conscience of the National Monuments Record; and Angela Horrocks in the Church Care Library in Church House (which deserves to be better known). Especial thanks are due to Geoff Brandwood for allowing me to use some of his superb photographs, and, as always, to Rosemary Hill, from whose home in Camberwell the prospect of St Giles's Church means much to us both. I am grateful to the Aurum Press and to Graham Coster in particular for asking me to write this short general, and I hope accessible, illustrated book about Scott's life and work. I had been interested in his architecture for many years, having first been introduced to it by the writings of John Betjeman and by a visit to the Midland Hotel at St Pancras, then threatened with demolition, organised by the Victorian Society in 1966 and led by the late Roderick Gradidge; and it was Rupert Sheldrake who, just a few years later, first took me to Kelham Hall. Finally, I should acknowledge the boon of e-Bay in being able easily to secure contemporary prints and old photographs of Scott's buildings.